NATIONAL TREATMENT
AND WTO DISPUTE SETTLEMENT

National Treatment and WTO Dispute Settlement

Adjudicating the Boundaries of Regulatory Autonomy

GAËTAN VERHOOSEL

·HART·
PUBLISHING
OXFORD – PORTLAND OREGON
2002

Hart Publishing
Oxford and Portland, Oregon

Published in North America (US and Canada) by
Hart Publishing c/o
International Specialized Book Services
5804 NE Hassalo Street
Portland, Oregon
97213-3644
USA

Distributed in the Netherlands, Belgium and Luxembourg by
Intersentia, Churchillaan 108
B2900 Schoten
Antwerpen
Belgium

Hart Publishing is a specialist legal publisher based in Oxford, England.
To order further copies of this book or to request a list of other
publications please write to:

Hart Publishing, Salter's Boatyard, Folly Bridge,
Abingdon Road, Oxford OX1 4LB
Telephone: +44 (0)1865 245533 or Fax: +44 (0)1865 794882
e-mail: mail@hartpub.co.uk
WEBSITE: http//www.hartpub.co.uk

British Library Cataloguing in Publication Data
Data Available
ISBN 1–84113–299–3 (hardback)

Typeset by Hope Services (Abingdon) Ltd.
Printed and bound in Great Britain on acid-free paper by
Biddles Ltd, www.biddles.co.uk

Voor papa en mama

Nere Emazte Maddirentzat

Acknowledgements

This book is based on my dissertation submitted in partial fulfilment of the requirements for the degree of Doctor of the Science of Law (J.S.D.) in the Faculty of Laws, Columbia University, New York. I sincerely thank the members of my all-star Advisory Committee at Columbia Law School: Professors George Bermann, Merit Janow and Petros Mavroidis. They were, in many respects, a guiding light. I have also greatly benefitted from comments by, and exchanges with Rob Howse (University of Michigan), Pieter Jan Kuijper (WTO Legal Affairs), Werner Zdouc (WTO Appellate Body) and Federico Ortino (European University Institute). Recalling our exchanges, I doubt that any of the above friends and colleagues share all the views expressed in this book, so the usual disclaimer applies.

The unconditional support of Professors Koen Lenaerts and Kurt Deketelaere at the University of Leuven was indispensable in the early stages of this project. This book should be a tribute to their generosity. Richard Hart and his team in Oxford gave shape to the features of the ideal publisher: vision, competence and efficiency.

Lastly, but far from least, an important thank you note to Columbia Law School and the Belgian American Educational Foundation for granting me the indispensable financial support while in residence at Columbia Law School during 1999–2000 as their *Herman Finkelstein* and *Francqui* Fellow, respectively.

Important, albeit obvious: the theses defended in this book took form prior to my appointment to the WTO's Legal Affairs Division, and all views expressed are strictly personal and cannot be attributed to the World Trade Organization, its Secretariat or its Members.

Gaëtan Verhoosel
Geneva
August 2001

Contents

1

Defining the Interface between WTO and Domestic Legal Orders through the Interpretation of National Treatment

A. INTRODUCTION

T HERE HAS BEEN a lot of talk lately, both popular and academic, about the impact of the World Trade Organization (WTO) on the domestic regulatory autonomy of WTO Members. Some have taken the view that this impact has in reality degenerated into an intrusion in domestic democratic decision-making processes by faceless international bureaucrats in Geneva. In particular, it has been suggested that the WTO, through the operation of its dispute settlement system, has at times crossed the line between trade liberalisation and deep market integration or negative harmonisation. Resulting claims regarding the "legitimacy" of the system and its adjudicators, i.e. dispute settlement panels and the Appellate Body, and the "constitutionalisation" of the WTO have become the subject of an intense debate.

This book attempts to contribute to that debate. It is submitted that WTO law and domestic legal regimes together make up a multi-layered legal order. As with any multi-layered legal order, two questions of federalism need to be answered to determine the proper functioning of that multi-layered legal order: (1) what can be required by the higher legal order from the lower legal order, and (2) who should decide on the allocation of decision-making power as between those two orders. In this book, we will argue that, in the WTO context, the answer to those questions depends greatly, if not entirely, upon the interpretation which one chooses to give to the National Treatment obligation and the fundamental non-discrimination principle it gives shape to in international trade relations.

It is submitted in that respect that facially origin-neutral domestic regulation often adversely affects imported products or foreign services/service suppliers, but that not all regulation inadvertently affecting those imports or services/service suppliers should therefore be considered a violation of the non-discrimination principle contained in the National Treatment provisions of GATT and GATS. The WTO has struggled with this question of how to distinguish between regulation which adversely affects imported products or foreign services/service suppliers, but has no protectionist motive, on the one hand, and covert protectionist measures, on the other. Along these lines, WTO dispute settlement panels have had particular problems delineating the jurisprudential concept of "*de facto* discrimination," i.e. discrimination in fact, not in law. In that respect, it is argued that the National Treatment obligation in GATT and GATS has turned out to be the key to determining the outer frontiers of the WTO system. National Treatment is the *gatekeeper* on the misty bridge between trade liberalisation and deep market integration. Interpreting that cornerstone obligation, therefore, is determining the constitutional function of the WTO.

In an attempt to define this constitutional function of the WTO, this book proposes an—what to some will seem audaciously—innovative interpretation of the concept of non-discrimination, as canvassed in the National Treatment obligations in the law of the World Trade Organization ("WTO Law"). Concretely, it develops the argument that, for a proper line to be drawn between trade liberalisation and deep integration or negative harmonisation, WTO adjudicators (i.e. dispute settlement panels and the Appellate Body) should apply an "*integrated necessity test*" under the provisions of the GATT and the GATS laying down their respective National Treatment obligations. Put another way, it is argued that *de facto* discrimination can only be revealed in an objective manner, and, hence, the borderline between trade liberalisation and deep market integration defined, by engaging in an analysis as to whether a particular regulatory instrument (1) specifically and adversely affects imported products or foreign services/service suppliers as compared with their like domestic counterparts, and (2) is necessary to achieve a purported legitimate policy goal, or, alternatively, whether other, less restrictive, regulatory means are available.

In order to demonstrate this point, the book starts by situating the reader in the debate. It provides an overview of the way in which GATT and GATS deal with domestic regulation, analytically surveying both treaty law and case law by panels and Appellate Body as regards the main legal parameters defining the interface between WTO and domestic law. These parameters are, apart from the National Treatment obligation, the legitimate policy exceptions and the concept of non-violation complaints. The book brings these different legal concepts together in an integrated analytical framework, explaining how each of them affects domestic regulatory autonomy and how they interact one with the next. It then goes on to unfold its main prescriptive argument, i.e. *why*

National Treatment should be understood to require a necessity test. Three major theories are developed to that effect.

First, a critical appraisal of the GATT/WTO panel and Appellate Body case law for each of said parameters leads us to conclude that this case law is rather intransparent and inconsistent. Problematic rulings by panels and/or the Appellate Body as regards the concept of "likeness", the determination of "protective application," and the relationship between National Treatment, on the one hand, and the legitimate policy objectives exception and non-violation provisions, on the other, are highlighted in this respect. Using a rules versus standards discourse, we then go on to demonstrate how the introduction of an integrated necessity test would remedy each of these shortcomings.

Second, we argue that a proper interpretation of the National Treatment provisions of GATT and GATS, in accordance with the provisions of the Vienna Convention on the Law of Treaties ("VCLT"), which guide panels and the Appellate Body in their interpretation of the WTO agreements, strongly mandates the use by panels of an integrated necessity test. Arguments to that effect are drawn from causation theory, textual and contextual analysis and effectiveness theory. In a parenthesis, we rebut anticipated criticism that constructs from EC law are being transposed into WTO law, showing that the relevant provisions in those two integration instruments are based on one and the same causation standard. To that end, we survey major case law by the European Court of Justice regarding free movement of goods and services and freedom of establishment, and cast it in the proposed causation mold.

Third, we submit that an integrated necessity test would do little more than implement the principle of good faith interpretation and performance of treaty obligations in public international law. According to this position, WTO Members perform their National Treatment obligation in good faith only when they try to avoid unnecessary adverse effects on imports. We then go on to develop a theory of optimal care in international trade, and argue that, under an economic analysis of the non-discrimination principle, this good faith obligation not to cause unnecessary adverse effects on imports, also constitutes the optimal level of care by a regulating WTO Member. An analogy with the *Hand Formula* in torts and a game theoretical model are used to clarify and support this proposition.

Finally, having explained at some length why the introduction of an integrated necessity test in National Treatment analysis should be supported, we briefly address the institutional aspect: can and should WTO panels scrutinise the "necessity" of domestic regulation, and what, if any, qualifications of the integrated necessity test should be considered for necessity to be "adjudicatable"?

A proper understanding of the normative arguments which we will develop throughout this book presupposes some basic knowledge about the way the multi-layered legal order made up of WTO and domestic legal regimes operates. Above we indicated that two questions are determinant in this respect: (1) what can be required by the higher legal order from the lower legal order, and (2) who should decide on the allocation of decision-making power as between those two orders. Below, we will use this template to sketch, very roughly, (1) the tension between the WTO and domestic regulation pursuing a variety of social policy goals, and (2) what the division of powers within the WTO as regards this "regulation of regulation" looks like.

B.   WTO AND DOMESTIC REGULATION: NATIONAL TREATMENT AS A GATEKEEPER

It is submitted that WTO Members' domestic regulatory systems are composed of a variety of policy measures "within the border," i.e. as opposed to the traditional border measures taking the form of tariffs and quotas. Members' diverging domestic regulation has become a focal point of trade liberalisation efforts during the past few years following three historical developments. First, the successful progressive reduction during the past fifty years of tariffs on industrial goods has increasingly revealed the presence of regulatory barriers, mainly in the form of technical, sanitary and phytosanitary standards.[1] Second, with the adoption of the GATS,[2] the trade liberalisation machinery was extended from trade in goods to trade and investment in services. Due to the heavily regulated nature of many service sectors, services trade and investment liberalisation is mainly hampered by regulatory heterogeneity as between Members.[3] And third, anti-competitive practices by private entities have increasingly been perceived as a barrier to market access. The finger was again pointed at regulatory heterogeneity, this time the divergence of domestic competition policies, and their enforcement.[4]

---

[1] To quote the adequate metaphor coined by Miles Kahler, "[t]he decades-long process of lowering trade barriers resembles the draining of a lake that reveals mountain peaks formerly concealed or (more pessimistically) the peeling of an onion that reveals innumerable layers of barriers." Miles Kahler, "Trade and Domestic Differences", in Suzanne Berger and Ronald Dore (eds.) *National Diversity and Global Capitalism* (1996), 298, 299.

[2] "General Agreement on Trade in Services", reprinted in WTO Secretariat (ed.) *The Results of the Uruguay Round of Multilateral Trade Negotiations* (1994) 325 (hereinafter *Uruguay Round Results*).

[3] See, for instance, Richard Snape, "Principles in Trade in Services", in Patrick Messerlin and Karl Sauvant (eds.) *The Uruguay Round. Services in the World Economy* (1990) 5, 7.

[4] See, for instance, Edward Graham, "Competition Policy and the New Trade Agenda", in Pierre Sauve and Americo B Zampetti (eds.) *New Dimensions of Market Access in a Globalising World Economy* (1995) 105.

These developments have brought to the fore the adverse impact which domestic regulatory heterogeneity between Members may have on the "effective equality of opportunities"[5] which the WTO system of agreements aims to establish. Very often, the domestic regulations at issue are origin-neutral and do not pursue a protectionist objective.[6] They simply are due to the historical differences in culture, values and preferences, as well as the different traditional approaches to regulation, which are inherent to each nation state. Such regulations, however, can effectively act as barriers to enhanced market access.[7] As a result, tension between the WTO system and regulatory autonomy of Members has grown considerably over the past decade. The WTO system is increasingly facing new demands of market access, aimed at reducing the obstacles resulting from Members' domestic regulatory heterogeneity. The proponents of this view submit:

> A further effect of globalisation is that it progressively enlarges the scope of trade policy preoccupations as more areas of national policy, heretofore regarded as mainly domestic, are now viewed as deeply affecting the ability of firms to compete internationally. [. . .] The trend is particularly evident with regard to "structural" differences among "national systems", such as business organisation and practices, corporate governance systems, capital and labour markets, regulatory regimes, including government-sanctioned monopolies, tax systems, standard-setting practices and a host of other industrial policy measures which strongly influence patterns of international business and conditions of market access and presence.[8]

We will term these new demands of market access "*market integration claims*," arguing that they call for the achievement of objectives ordinarily dissociated from trade liberalisation goals, and rather related to the process of international market integration.[9] As observed by the

---

[5] This phrase was introduced by the panel report in *United States—Section 337 of the Tariff Act of 1930* (L/6439, adopted 7 November 1989, BISD 36S/345, para. 5.11), interpreting the National Treatment obligation of GATT Art. III:4: "[. . .] The words 'treatment no less favourable' in paragraph 4 [of GATT Art. III] call for effective equality of opportunities for imported products in respect of the application of laws, regulations and requirements affecting internal sale, offering for sale, purchase, transportation, distribution or use of products. [. . .]"

[6] Jim Rollo and Alan Winters, "Domestic Regulation and Trade: Subsidiarity and Governance Challenges for the WTO", paper presented at the WTO/World Bank Conference on Developing Countries and the Millenium Round, Geneva, 20–21 September 1999, 1 (on file with the author).

[7] See, for instance, Daniel Farber and Robert Hudec, "Free Trade and the Regulatory State: A GATT's-Eye View of the Dormant Commerce Clause", 47 *Vanderbilt Law Review* (1994) 1401, 1402.

[8] Americo B Zampetti and Pierre Sauve, "New Dimensions of Market Access: An Overview", in Sauve and Zampetti (eds.) *New Dimensions of Market Access in a Globalising World Economy* (1995) 13, 16.

[9] For the purpose of this paper, by trade liberalisation we will understand a process aimed at reducing tariffs and quotas as between nations, and supported by MFN and national treatment obligations. By market integration, we refer to a process which, in

proponents of market integration claims, the WTO system is historically ill-equipped to meet those demands.[10] This is, of course, due to the fact that the WTO system, with its quasi-global membership, aims at—and provides the legal tools for—trade liberalisation rather than "deep" market integration,[11] as evidenced by the wording of its Preamble.[12] This limited object and purpose of the WTO Agreement informs the interpretation of all annexed agreements,[13] in particular their provisions laying down disciplines on domestic regulation.[14]

addition to trade liberalisation, aims at the abolition of all obstacles, both at and behind the border, to freedom of movement for all factors—including persons, services and capital—by introducing convergence and/or harmonisation of domestic economic, monetary and social regulatory policies. See Peter Robson, *The Economics of International Integration* 4th edn. (1998) 63, 72. See also Bernard Hoekman and Petros Mavroidis, "Competition, Competition Policy and the GATT", 17 *The World Economy* (1994) 121, 124, who distinguish along the same lines between "free market access" and "economic integration".

[10] Americo B. Zampetti and Pierre Sauve, *supra* n. 8, 16.

[11] Bernard Hoekman and Petros Mavroidis, *supra* n. 9, 125. Peter Robson, *supra* n. 9, 61.

[12] According to the Preamble to the Marrakesh Agreement establishing the World Trade Organisation, the WTO system mainly aims at "expanding the production of and trade in goods and services." This language can easily be contrasted with the unique market integration project of the European Community announced by Arts. 2 and 3 of the Treaty of Rome. These provisions state that the European Community shall have as its task, by establishing an internal market characterised by the abolition of obstacles to the free movement of goods, persons, services and capital and an economic and monetary union, to promote throughout the Community a harmonious and balanced development of economic activities, sustainable and non-inflationary growth respecting the environment, a high degree of convergence of economic performance, a high level of employment and of social protection, the raising of the standard of living and quality of life, and economic and social cohesion and solidarity among Member States. See also Jim Rollo and Alan Winters, *supra* n. 16, 14: "Overall therefore it would be surprising if the EU experience were to provide a ready-made template for global regulation and liberalisation." For a pre-WTO assessment along these lines, the gist of which remains valid, see Claus-Dieter Ehlermann and Gianluigi Campogrande, "Rules on Services in the EEC: A Model for Negotiating World-Wide Rules?" in Ernst Ulrich Petersmann and Meinhard Hilf (eds.) *The New GATT Round of Multilateral Trade Negotiations* (1990) 481, 482–483.

[13] The Appellate Body considers Arts. 31 and 32 of the Vienna Convention on the Law of Treaties to form part of the "customary rules of interpretation of public international law" which it is directed, by Art. 3(2) of the Understanding on Rules and Procedures Governing the settlement of Disputes ("DSU"), to apply in seeking to clarify the provisions of the various agreements making up the WTO system (Appellate Body report on *United States— Standards for Reformulated Conventional Gasoline*, WT/DS2/AB/R, adopted 20 May 1996). According to Art. 31, a treaty shall be interpreted in good faith in accordance with the ordinary meaning to be given to the terms of the treaty in their context and in the light of its object and purpose. According to the Appellate Body, "[a]s [. . .] preambular language reflects the intentions of negotiators of the WTO Agreement, [. . .] it must add colour, texture and shading to our interpretation of the agreements annexed to the WTO agreement [. . .]." Appellate Body report on *United States—Import Prohibition of Certain Shrimp and Shrimp Products* (WT/DS58/AB/R, adopted 6 November 1998), para. 43.

[14] "The rules of the [GATT] primarily aim at the reduction of barriers between markets, not at the harmonisation of competitive conditions in markets. They therefore impose in principle only constraints on trade policies, but leave the contracting parties free to conduct their domestic policies." Frieder Roessler, "Diverging Domestic Policies and Multilateral Trade Integration", in Jagdish Bhagwati and Robert Hudec (eds.) *Fair Trade and Harmonisation* vol. 2 (1996) 1.

Trade liberalisation and market integration, however, are not clearly delineated stages in economic integration. Rather, they sit on a continuum and one seems to shade seamlessly into the other. There is, nonetheless supposed to be a gatekeeper on this misty bridge between trade liberalisation and market integration: this is the principle of non-discrimination, canvassed in the National Treatment obligation.

Defining National Treatment boils down to performing an arbitrage between these stages of integration. Defining National Treatment means determining the constitutional function of the WTO. Arguably, once an international legal framework is no longer permissive of non-discriminatory regulation adversely affecting the competitive opportunities of foreign goods or services, it has embarked on a process of deregulation and deep market integration. As Petros Mavroidis has once put it,[15] "WTO law is about non-discrimination, *not* about deregulation!" But, while this one-liner surely appears to be vested with the authority of dogma,[16] it also begs a fundamental question: what should we understand by "non-discrimination," or "National Treatment"? Does it suffice for the competitive conditions of foreign goods and services to be adversely affected by the existence of domestic regulation for the latter to be discriminatory, even if these effects are the results of fortuitous circumstances?[17] Or should we somehow take into account the fact that domestic regulation, even when it is on its face origin-neutral, imposes often a heavier burden on foreign suppliers, because they are simply "caught by surprise," become subject to redundant regulatory requirements, incur loss of scale economies, information costs, or conformity assessment costs?[18]

In this book we will argue that very sound normative policy and legal arguments exist to suggest that National Treatment should and can only be defined by referring to the necessity of domestic regulation.

---

[15] During the opening lecture of the WTO law class taught by Professor Mavroidis at Columbia Law School in Fall 1999.

[16] Compare this statement to one by Professor Frieder Roessler: "The GATT has now been supplemented by agreements annexed to the Agreement establishing the World Trade Organisation [. . .] that go beyond the mere prohibition of discrimination and establish requirements for domestic regulations, that is, regulations equally applicable to domestic and foreign goods, services and service suppliers. The distinction between foreign trade policies, in respect of which governments accept to be bound, and domestic economic policies, which they may conduct autonomously, is no longer being made." Frieder Roessler, "Increasing Market Access under Regulatory Heterogeneity: The Strategies of the World Trade Organisation", in OECD (ed.) *Regulatory Reform and International Market Openness* (1996) 117.

[17] See, for instance, David Vogel, *Trading Up: Consumer and Environmental Regulation in a Global Economy* (1993) 14: "If all regulations that disadvantaged importers were classified as non-tariff barriers, then virtually all regulations could be considered protectionist."

[18] Alan Sykes, "The (Limited) Role of Regulatory Harmonisation in International Goods and Services Markets", 2 *Journal of International Economic Law* (1999) 49, 53–56.

C. IS NECESSITY "ADJUDICATABLE"?

Having made this case for equating National Treatment with necessity on the basis of substantive policy and legal arguments, however, we will subsequently admit that the implementation of such a necessity test may potentially be troublesome in the current institutional setting. This question of implementation naturally shades into the second aspect of federalism referred to earlier, by asking *who* can and should decide whether a particular domestic regulation is "necessary", once it has been argued that such an integrated necessity test is the proper criterion to define the National Treatment obligations of GATT and GATS. Put simply, can and should this task be left to the "judiciary"—the WTO ad hoc adjudicators—and what legitimacy concerns, if any, would this raise?

The lawyer could argue in this respect that Article 3:2 of the DSU[19] and Article IX:2 of the WTO Agreement[20], read together, should be explained as a political shot by the WTO membership across the bow of WTO adjudicators, exhorting them not to engage in any sort of "judicial activism" or "judicial policy-making." The collective WTO Membership, i.e. over 140 sovereign states or customs territories, thus maintains a monopoly on the adoption and amendment of multilateral trade-related rules, and it does so by consensus, through traditional treaty bargaining. Below, however, we will argue that the interpretation of National Treatment we propose is simply the proper one, and not an "activist" one.

But, more importantly, the policy maker will wonder whether this is the right solution within the current institutional framework of the WTO. It can be noted in this respect that, unlike the European Community, where market integration has been and is being pursued using two different tracks—"negative"[21] and "positive"[22]—the WTO system is

---

[19] This provision reads: "The dispute settlement system of the WTO is a central element in providing security and predictability to the multilateral trading system. The Members recognise that it serves to preserve the rights and obligations of Members under the covered agreements, and to clarify the existing provisions of those agreements in accordance with customary rules of interpretation of public international law. *Recommendations and rulings of the DSB cannot add to or diminish the rights and obligations provided in the covered agreements.*" (emphasis added)

[20] This provision reads: "The Ministerial Conference and the General Council shall have *the exclusive authority* to adopt interpretations of this Agreement and of the Multilateral Trade Agreements. In the case of an interpretation of a Multilateral Trade Agreement in Annex 1, they shall exercise their authority on the basis of a recommendation by the Council overseeing the functioning of that Agreement. The decision to adopt an interpretation shall be taken by a three-fourths majority of the Members." (emphasis added)

[21] It has often been observed that the judicial activism of the European Court of Justice (ECJ) has enabled it to interpret the Treaty of Rome's provisions on the free movement of goods and services and the freedom of establishment as including a prohibition of origin-neutral (which the ECJ refers to as "indistinctly applicable") measures which act as barriers to intra-Community trade and investment, and requiring mutual recognition of standards

endowed with only some embryonic features of positive integration,[23] remaining mainly a system based on negative integration. Some authors believe this should remain so in the future as well. Michael Trebilcock and Robert Howse, for instance, have forcefully opined that "trade regimes and institutions should largely confine themselves to a more fully elaborated principle of non-discrimination with well-defined exceptions thereto—that is, a concept of negative rather than positive integration."[24]

Although we will argue, on the basis of our conclusions in this book, that an integrated necessity test may, subject to certain requirements, very well qualify for such a "more fully elaborated principle of non-discrimination," the question remains as to whether such an elaboration can and should be left to WTO ad hoc arbitrators. Therefore, independently from the (real or perceived) substantive merits of our proposal, we will address the issue whether WTO adjudicators can and should inquire into the necessity of domestic regulation.

D. OVERVIEW

In the remainder of this book, we will proceed as follows. First, in chapter two, we will summarily describe the rules of WTO law—both as regards GATT and GATS—which govern Members' regulatory autonomy. We will then, in chapter three, present an overview of the

---

under certain conditions. This judicial application of the EC Treaty's freedom provisions, which is aimed at the abolishment of intra-Community trade barriers is commonly referred to as a process of "negative integration." See, for instance, PJG Kapteyn and P. Verloren Van Themaat, *Introduction to the Law of the European Communities* (1998) 584.

[22] The Community legislator has zealously carried out its mandate provided in the Treaty of Rome—and continues to do so—to introduce an "approximation of laws," i.e. some degree of harmonisation of the domestic laws and regulations of the Member States. This process of "positive integration" was given new impetus with the Commission's Internal Market program and its "new approach" of minimum harmonisation. See *Commission of the European Communities, Completing the Internal Market* (1985), white paper, COM(85)310 final. Joseph Weiler has described the dynamic interface between the ECJ and the other Community institutions, the negative and the positive track, throughout the development of the European Communities in his "Transformation of Europe." Joseph Weiler, "The Transformation of Europe", 100 *Yale Law Journal* (1991) 2403. In particular, using the exit & voice discourse, Weiler described how the ECJ in the foundational period had "closed selective exit," i.e. had curtailed the ability of the Member States to practice a selective application of the *acquis communautaire*, by establishing the doctrines of direct effect, supremacy, implied powers and human rights. *Ibid.*, 2412–2430.

[23] See, for instance, the provisions of the TBT and SPS agreements regarding international standardisation, Art. VI:4 GATS mandating the Council on Trade in Services to negotiate standardisation, or the Basic Telecom Reference Paper.

[24] Michael Trebilcock and Robert Howse, "Trade Liberalisation and Regulatory Diversity: Reconciling Competitive Markets with Competitive Politics", 6 *European Journal of Law and Economics* (1998) 5, 31.

GATT/WTO case law which has meant to give interpretation to these legal rules. Both chapters two and three are descriptive/analytical. On the one hand, they are meant to be didactic, introducing readers who are less familiar with the debate, to the basic premises upon which we will build in chapter five. On the other hand, they also have a "photo-function": the reader should have a complete, accurate and clear picture of the past and current case law before we can critically assess it. Chapter four will be the bridge between description and prescription, both an occasion for stocktaking and announcing our main conceptual move. Finally, in chapter five, we will explain in some detail why we think that National Treatment should be read as requiring a necessity test, outlining a variety of arguments to support our thesis. In that section, we will also briefly touch upon the institutional issue, i.e. can and should WTO ad hoc adjudicators legitimately make sensible decisions about the necessity of a Member's domestic regulation, and what qualifications, if any, of the necessity test, are required for that matter?

2

The Building Blocks: GATT Rules on Domestic Regulation and The 1994 Transplant to Services

A. THE GATT SYSTEM FOR POLICING DOMESTIC REGULATION: BASICS

GATT "REGULATES REGULATION" on several accounts, but it only addresses its substance in one respect, and that is in the requirement of non-discrimination. It provides rules on the publication[1] and administration[2] of domestic regulation, but these do not affect the substance of domestic regulation *per se*.[3] The only provisions addressing the substance of domestic regulation are Articles I and III, laying down the Most Favoured Nation (MFN) and National Treatment obligations,

---

[1] GATT Art. X:1 provides that "[l]aws, regulations, judicial decisions and administrative rulings of general application, made effective by any contracting party, [. . .] affecting their sale, distribution, transportation, insurance, warehousing inspection, exhibition, processing, mixing or other use, shall be published promptly in such a manner as to enable governments and traders to become acquainted with them. [. . .]" In its report on *EC—Measures Affecting the Importation of Certain Poultry Products* (WT/DS69/R, adopted 23 July 1998), para. 269, the panel found in this respect that licenses issued to a specific company or applied to a specific shipment cannot be considered to be a measure "of general application," approvingly referring to the panel's statement in *United States— Restrictions on Imports of Cotton and Man-made Fibre Underwear* (WT/DS24/R, adopted 25 February 1997), para. 7.65. The Appellate Body upheld this finding on appeal (WT/DS69/AB/R, adopted 25 February 1997), para. 113.

[2] The Appellate Body has stated in *EC—Regime for the Importation, Sale and Distribution of Bananas* (WT/DS27/AB/R, adopted 25 September 1997, para. 200) that "[t]he text of Art. X:3(a) clearly indicates that the requirements of "uniformity, impartiality and reasonableness" do not apply to the laws, regulations, decisions and rulings *themselves*, but rather to the *administration* of those laws, regulations, decisions and rulings. The context of Art. X:3(a) within Art. X, which is entitled "Publication and Administration of Trade Regulations", and a reading of the other paragraphs of Art. X, make it clear that Art. X applies to the *administration* of laws, regulations, decisions and rulings. To the extent that the laws, regulations, decisions and rulings themselves are discriminatory, they can be examined for their consistency with the relevant provisions of the GATT 1994."

[3] In its report on *EC—Measures Affecting the Importation of Certain Poultry Products*, *supra*, para. 115, the Appellate Body has stated that "to the extent [an] appeal relates to the *substantive content* of the EC rules themselves, and not to their *publication* or *administration*, that appeal falls outside the scope of Art. X of the GATT 1994. The WTO-consistency of such substantive content must be determined by reference to provisions of the covered agreements other than Art. X of the GATT 1994." (original emphasis).

respectively. For the purpose of this chapter, however, only Article III is of relevance.[4] The reason for this is that their underlying rationale is different. Whereas MFN has a "multilateralisation" objective, the aim of National Treatment is "to prevent domestic tax and regulatory policies from being used as protectionist measures that would defeat the purpose of tariff bindings,"[5] and to provide "equal conditions of competition once goods had been cleared through customs."[6] The focus of this book will be on superficially origin-neutral measures which are said to adversely affect the competitive conditions of *all* foreign products/ services, as compared to domestic products/services, without distinguishing between various foreign products/services according to their respective country of origin.

This basic injunction not to discriminate between domestic and imported goods as regards their tax and regulatory treatment must be read in connection with GATT Articles XX and XXIII:1(b). Article XX provides the well-known list of grounds for exemption from GATT obligations, including Article III. Its aim is to allow Members to act inconsistently with their GATT obligations, including National Treatment, when (1) a certain degree of causality between the regulation and the achievement of a legitimate policy goal can be demonstrated,[7] and (2) the regulation does not constitute a means of arbitrary or unjustifiable discrimination or a disguised restriction on international trade.[8]

---

[4] The text of paras. 1, 2 and 4 of GATT Art. III reads:

"1. The contracting parties recognise that internal taxes and other internal charges, and laws, regulations and requirements affecting the internal sale, offering for sale, purchase, transportation, distribution or use of products, and internal quantitative regulations requiring the mixture, processing or use of products in specified amounts or proportions, should not be applied to imported or domestic products so as to afford protection to domestic production.

2. The products of the territory of any contracting party imported into the territory of any other contracting party shall not be subject, directly or indirectly, to internal taxes or other internal charges of any kind in excess of those applied, directly or indirectly, to like domestic products. Moreover, no contracting party shall otherwise apply internal taxes or other internal charges to imported or domestic products in a manner contrary to the principles set forth in para. 1.

[...]

4. The products of the territory of any contracting party imported into the territory of any other contracting party shall be accorded treatment no less favourable than that accorded to like products of national origin in respect of all laws, regulations and requirements affecting their internal sale, offering for sale, purchase, transportation, distribution or use. The provisions of this paragraph shall not prevent the application of differential internal transportation charges which are based exclusively on the economic operation of the means of transport and not on the nationality of the product."

[5] John H. Jackson, *The World Trading System* (1997) 213.

[6] Report of the panel on *Italian Discrimination Against Imported Agricultural Machinery* (L833, adopted 23 October 1958, BISD 7S/60), para. 5.

[7] The regulation should either be "necessary" (paras. a, b, d and i), "relating to" (paras. c, e and g), "for the protection of" (para. f), "in pursuance of" (para. h), or "essential to" (para. j).

[8] The so-called chapeau of Art. XX.

Article XXIII:1(b) has to be read in the light of this considerable regulatory freedom which the GATT drafters have left to Members. According to this provision, if any contracting party should consider that any benefit accruing to it directly or indirectly under GATT is being nullified or impaired or that the attainment of any objective of GATT is being impeded as the result of "the application by another contracting party of any measure, whether or not it conflicts with the provisions of this Agreement," that contracting party may seek redress[9] through the dispute settlement system by filing a so-called non-violation complaint. One author has described the function of non-violation complaints in relation to Members' regulatory autonomy as follows:

> As a consequence of the domestic policy autonomy which the WTO Members enjoy, the benefits that they expect to obtain by negotiating tariff concessions [. . .] can be nullified or impaired through new domestic regulatory measures that are consistent with the WTO agreements. To encourage WTO Members to exchange nevertheless such concessions [. . .], they were given a right of redress when a benefit they could reasonably have expected to accrue to them under a concession [. . .] is being nullified or impaired as a result of a legal measure.[10]

During the Uruguay Round, the Tokyo Round Standards Code was revised and multilateralised to become the WTO Agreement on Technical Barriers to Trade (TBT). At the same time, the Agreement on Sanitary and Phytosanitary Standards (SPS) was adopted. Both agreements aim at enhancing disciplines on the adoption and application of technical standards in order to avoid them constituting unnecessary obstacles to trade in goods. Without excessively generalising, it can be said in fairness that both TBT and SPS: (1) regulate *how* covered regulations should be adopted;[11] (2) lay down a *necessity* test for these measures;[12] (3) favour *international standardisation* or *harmonisation*[13] and *mutual recognition*;[14] (4) regulate *conformity assessment*[15] or *control and approval*[16] procedures; and (5) provide obligations as regards *transparency*.[17]

---

[9] The complaining Member can only obtain from the panel or Appellate Body a recommendation to the Member concerned to make a "mutually satisfactory adjustment." There is no obligation to withdraw the measure (Art. 26:1(b) DSU).

[10] Frieder Roessler, "Increasing Market Access under Regulatory Heterogeneity: The Strategies of the World Trade Organisation", in OECD (ed.) in *Regulatory Reform and International Market Openness* (1996) 126–127.

[11] TBT Art. 3, 4. SPS Art. 5.

[12] TBT Art. 2.2–2.3. SPS Art. 2.1–2.2 and 5.6. Note that the list of legitimate objectives is not exhaustive under TBT, whereas it is under SPS.

[13] TBT Art. 2.4, 2.5, 2.6. SPS Art. 3.

[14] TBT Arts. 2.7, 6. SPS Art. 4.

[15] TBT Arts. 5, 7, 8.

[16] SPS Art. 8, Annex C.

[17] TBT Arts. 2.9–2.12, 10. SPS Art. 7, Annex B.

In addition, both agreements impose disciplines on superficially origin-neutral domestic regulation which goes beyond the above requirements. The TBT Agreement, on the one hand, goes further than the traditional, Article XX-like, necessity test by allowing panels in the process to "tak[e] into account the risks non-fulfilment [of a legitimate objective] would create."[17a] According to some, this would effectively allow panels not only to conduct a "least-restrictive means" analysis, but also to perform a "balancing" test, weighing the costs of the regulation against the benefits of the legitimate objective.[18] The SPS Agreement, on the other hand, imposes important disciplines as regards the scientific basis of sanitary and phytosanitary standards.[19]

B. THE GOODS–SERVICES TRANSPLANT

Trade in services is conceptually quite different from trade in goods.[20] Whereas traded goods are tangible and storable, traded services are intangible and must often be produced and consumed simultaneously.[21] Goods are traded by physically crossing national borders, whereas services can be delivered in various ways: cross-border provision through telecommunication media or postal services, cross-border movement of the service provider to the country of the consumer, and cross-border movement of the consumer to the country of the service provider.[22] Whereas barriers to trade in goods can take the form of both tariff and non-tariff barriers, barriers to services trade are primarily of a regulatory

---

[17a] See TBT Art 2.2. As this book was going to print, the panel on *European Communities—Trade Description of Sardines* (WT/DS231) was hearing a case involving claims made under TBT Art. 2.2. Unless the parties settle their differences before the panel issues its final report, such report could become the first adopted panel report to propose an interpretation of the substantive disciplines of the TBT Agreement.

[18]   Alan Sykes, *Product Standards for Internationally Integrated Goods Markets* (1995) 78.

[19]   See, generally, David Wirth, "The Role of Science in the Uruguay Round and NAFTA Trade Disciplines", 27 *Cornell International Law Journal* (1994) 817. The SPS provisions have already been repeatedly applied by Panels and Appellate Body: *Japan—Measures Affecting Agricultural Products* (WT/DS76/R and WT/DS76/AB/R, adopted 19 March 1999), *EC—Measures concerning Meat and Meat Products (Hormones)* (WT/DS26/R and WT/DS26/AB, adopted 13 February 1998), *Australia—Measures affecting Imports of Salmon* (WT/DS18/R and WT/DS18/AB/R, adopted 6 November 1998).

[20]   We believe this to be a majority view. Some authors have argued, however, that "[c]ontrary ro the wide belief which has dominated the drafting of GATS, services are not intrinsically different from goods." Patrick Messerlin, *Regulatory Reforms in Services and Commercial Policy: The Case of Developing Countries*, mimeo, (1999), p. 2.

[21]   Bimal Ghosh, *Gains from Global Linkages: Trade in Services and Movement of Persons* (1997) 6, who notes, however, that these conceptual differences do not allow to adequately define services.

[22]   Bernard Hoekman and Pierre Sauve, *Liberalizing Trade in Services* 3 (World Bank Discussion Paper No 243, 1994).

nature (quantitative restrictions, standards, qualification, market regulation), situated within the border.[23]

Given these important conceptual differences, concerns had been expressed that an outright transplant of the disciplines of the GATT multilateral framework to services trade could prove to be somewhat simplistic and fairly problematic.[24] The Group on Negotiation of Services (GNS) struggled indeed with this idea at the beginning of its mandate and thereafter.[25] It was nevertheless decided to take the GATT provisions as a basis and try and tailor them to the particularities of services trade. Considering that tariff barriers are quasi-non-existent as regards services trade, a structure needed to be designed allowing the scheduling of concessions along the lines of GATT tariff concessions. This was reflected in Article XVI on Market Access listing six categories of measures (five of which take the form of quantitative restrictions) which Members are not allowed to apply in sectors for which they have scheduled a market access commitment, unless they provide otherwise in their schedule.[26]

As regards the interface between trade liberalisation and domestic regulation, the Articles III-XX-XXIII:1(b) structure of GATT was cut and pasted into the GATS, with some textual amendments often reflecting established interpretations by GATT dispute settlement practice (GATS

---

[23] *Ibid.*, at 7. The authors distinguish between (1) measures that are quantity-based; (2) those that are price-based; (3) those that require physical or corporate presence in a market; (4) those relating to standards, certification requirements and industry-specific regulations; and (5) measures relating to government procurement and subsidisation. See also Tycho HE Stahl, "Liberalizing International Trade in Services: The Case for Sidestepping the GATT", 19 *Yale Journal of International Law* (1994) 405, 411.

[24] John H. Jackson, *supra* n. 29, at 157 with regard to MFN, and at 214 with regard to National Treatment. See also Mario Marconini, "The Uruguay Round Negotiations on Services: An Overview", in Patrick Messerlin and Karl Sauvant (eds.) *The Uruguay Round. Services in the World Economy* (1990) 19, 21; Friedl Weiss, "The General Agreement on Trade in Services 1994", 32 *Common Market Law Review* (1995) 1177, 1205.

[25] Terence Stewart, *The Uruguay Round: A Negotiating History* (1993), 2360, 2365.

[26] The six categories are:

(a) limitations on the number of service suppliers whether in the form of numerical quotas, monopolies, exclusive service suppliers or the requirements of an economic needs test;

(b) limitations on the total value of service transactions or assets in the form of numerical quotas or the requirement of an economic needs test;

(c) limitations on the total number of service operations or on the total quantity of service output expressed in terms of designated numerical units in the form of quotas or the requirement of an economic needs test;

(d) limitations on the total number of natural persons that may be employed in a particular service sector or that a service supplier may employ and who are necessary for, and directly related to, the supply of a specific service in the form of numerical quotas or the requirement of an economic needs test;

(e) measures which restrict or require specific types of legal entity or joint venture through which a service supplier may supply a service; and

(f) limitations on the participation of foreign capital in terms of maximum percentage limit on foreign shareholding or the total value of individual or aggregate foreign investment.

Articles XVII, XIV and XXIII:3[27]). Of course, unlike GATT Article III, GATS Article XVII[28] on National Treatment is, like GATS Article XVI, a specific commitment, i.e. only applicable to the extent scheduled.[29] GATS Article XIV mirrors the provision of GATT Article XX, in that it allows members to take measures inconsistent with their obligations under GATS but necessary to achieve certain legitimate policy objectives,[30] and the chapeau has been drafted in identical terms.[31]

GATS Article VI has been said to mirror the TBT-SPS approach for services trade.[32] Paragraphs 1, 2 and 3 of Article VI provide for disciplines as

---

[27] There are, however, important differences between non-violation under GATT and non-violation under GATS. See further below.

[28] The text of GATS Art. XVII reads:

"1. In the sectors inscribed in its Schedule, and subject to any conditions and qualifications set out therein, each Member shall accord to services and service suppliers of any other Member, in respect of all measures affecting the supply of services, treatment no less favourable than that it accords to its own like services and service suppliers.[10]

2. A Member may meet the requirement of para. 1 by according to services and service suppliers of any other Member, either formally identical treatment or formally different treatment to that it accords to its own like services and service suppliers.

3. Formally identical or formally different treatment shall be considered to be less favourable if it modifies the conditions of competition in favour of services or service suppliers of the Member compared to like services or service suppliers of any other Member."

The original footnote 10 to para. 1 provides that "[s]pecific commitments assumed under this Article shall not be construed to require any Member to compensate for any inherent competitive disadvantages which result from the foreign character of the relevant services or service suppliers." The second and third paragraph have been inspired by GATT dispute settlement practice. The wording of para. 2 draws upon the GATT Panel report on *United States—Section 337 of the Tariff Act of 1930* (BISD 36S/345, adopted 7 November 1989, para. 5.11). Para. 3 was inspired by the GATT Panel report on *Italian Discrimination Against Imported Agricultural Machinery* (BISD 7, 7S/60, adopted 23 October 1958, para. 12).

[29] First paragraph of GATS Art. XVII:1.

[30] Regulation can be either (a) necessary to protect public morals or to maintain public order; or (b) necessary to protect human, animal or plant life or health; or (c) necessary to secure compliance with laws or regulations which are not inconsistent with the provisions of this Agreement (prevention of deceptive and fraudulent practices, effects of a default on services contracts, the protection of the privacy, safety); or (d) inconsistent with Art. XVII, provided that the difference in treatment is aimed at ensuring the equitable or effective imposition or collection of direct taxes in respect of services or service suppliers of other Members; or (e) inconsistent with Art. II, provided that the difference in treatment is the result of an agreement on the avoidance of double taxation or provisions on the avoidance of double taxation in any other international agreement or arrangement by which the Member is bound. A footnote to para. (a) clarifies that the public order exception may be invoked only where a genuine and sufficiently serious threat is posed to one of the fundamental interests of society.

[31] In addition to these general exceptions, there are also sector-specific provisions laying down exceptions. See Art. 2 of the Annex on Financial Services which allows members to adopt measures for prudential reasons, and Art. 5(d) of the Annex on Telecommunications which allows Members to adopt measures necessary to ensure the security and confidentiality of messages, subject to the requirement that such measures are not applied in a manner which would constitute a means of arbitrary or unjustifiable discrimination or a disguised restriction on trade in services.

[32] Joel Trachtman, "Trade in Financial Services under GATS, NAFTA and the EC: A Regulatory Jurisdiction Analysis", 34 *Columbia Journal of Transnational Law* (1995) 37.

regards the administration of domestic regulation, the maintenance or institution of adequate judicial tribunals or procedures, and the administration of authorisation applications, respectively. Only paragraphs 4 and 5, however, touch upon the substance of domestic regulation. Paragraph 4 mandates the Council for Trade in Services, with a view to ensuring that measures relating to qualification requirements and procedures, technical standards and licensing requirements do not constitute unnecessary barriers to trade in services to develop any necessary disciplines. Such disciplines shall aim to ensure that such requirements are, *inter alia*, (1) based on objective and transparent criteria, such as competence and the ability to supply the service; (2) not more burdensome than necessary to ensure the quality of the service; and (3) in the case of licensing procedures, not in themselves a restriction on the supply of the service.

This task was originally assigned to the Working Party on Professional Services (WPPS), but was recently reassigned to a newly established Working Party on Domestic Regulation (WPDR).[33] Not much progress has been made to date by the WPPS: only at the end of 1998, the Council on Trade in Services adopted the "Disciplines on Domestic Regulation in the Accountancy Sector" negotiated in the WPPS.[34] The *Disciplines* "are to be applicable" to Members who have entered specific commitments on accountancy in their schedules. No later than the conclusion of the current services negotiations, the *Disciplines* "are intended to be integrated into GATS." Until then, "Members shall, to the fullest extent consistent with their existing legislation, not take measures which would be inconsistent with these disciplines."[35] The WPDR, on the other hand, has focused its discussions on the development of horizontal rules, in particular a cross-the-board necessity test.[36]

Paragraph 5 of Article VI provides that in sectors in which a Member has undertaken specific commitments, pending the entry into force of disciplines developed in these sectors pursuant to paragraph 4, that Member shall not apply licensing and qualification requirements and technical standards that nullify or impair such specific commitments in a manner which does not comply with the criteria outlined in paragraph 4 and could not reasonably have been expected of that Member at the time the specific commitments in those sectors were made. In determining whether a Member is in conformity with the obligation

[33] Decision on Domestic Regulation, adopted by the Council on Trade in Services on 26 April 1999 (S/L/70). The Working Party must report to the Council with recommendations no later than the conclusion of the next services negotiations.
[34] Decision on Disciplines relating to the Accountancy Sector, adopted 15 December 1998 (S/L/63). The text of the *Disciplines* are contained in document S/WPPS/W/21.
[35] *Ibid.*, para. 2–3.
[36] See the WT/S/WPDR documents available from the WTO website.

under this provision, account shall be taken of international standards of relevant international organisations applied by that Member. As we will explain below, paragraph 5 has in fact "violationised" a non-violation complaint.

3

How They Were Construed:
The Case Law on National Treatment,
Legitimate Policy Exceptions and
Non-Violation under GATT and GATS

A. THE DEFINITION OF THE SCOPE OF NATIONAL TREATMENT UNDER GATT AND
GATS BY PANELS AND APPELLATE BODY

T HE WORDING OF the National Treatment obligations in GATT and GATS has several key elements in common which define their respective scope. The language in both provisions prohibits (a) either all laws, regulations and requirements or all measures, (b) affecting either the internal sale, offering for sale, purchase, transportation, distribution or use of goods or the supply of services, (c) which accord less favourable treatment to either foreign goods or foreign services/service suppliers, (d) than to either like domestic goods or domestic like services/service suppliers. This section will review the relevant case law for each of these constitutive elements.

1. Scope *Ratione Formae*: "All laws, regulations and requirements" and "all measures"

As for forms of government action which are potentially caught by the National Treatment obligation in GATT and GATS, Panels have traditionally refused to read the phrase "all laws, regulations and requirements" in a restrictive manner, preferring a functional approach instead. It appears from the GATT case law on the record that: (1) in judging whether a measure is contrary to obligations under Article III:4, it is not relevant whether it applies across-the-board or only in isolated cases;[1]

---

[1] Panel report on *Canada—Administration of the Foreign Investment Review Act* (L/5504, BISD 30S/140, adopted 7 February 1984).

(2) private contractual obligations entered into by investors should not adversely affect the rights which contracting parties, including contracting parties not involved in the dispute, possess under Article III:4 of the General Agreement;[2] (3) the comprehensive coverage of "all laws, regulations or requirements affecting" the internal sale, etc. of imported products suggests that not only requirements which an enterprise is legally bound to carry out, but also those which an enterprise voluntarily accepts in order to obtain an advantage from the government, constitute "requirements" within the meaning of that provision;[3] (4) enforcement procedures cannot be separated from the substantive provisions they serve to enforce and are also within the scope of Article III.[4]

As regards GATS practice, the scope of the "measures" referred to in GATS Article XVII:1 has, as of the time of writing, only been defined *ratione materiae*, not *ratione formae*. Put another, way, dispute settlement bodies have had to deal with the interpretation of the phrase "affecting the supply of services," rather than the question which particular form the actual "measures" could take.

2. Scope *Ratione Materiae*: "Affecting"

The panel report on *Italian Discrimination against Imported Agricultural Machinery* is, to our knowledge, the only adopted GATT panel report to have addressed the interpretation of the phrase "affected" *per se*. In the opinion of the panel, the selection of the word "affecting" implied that the drafters of the Article intended to cover in paragraph 4 not only the laws and regulations which directly governed the conditions of sale or purchase but also any laws or regulations which might adversely modify the conditions of competition between the domestic and imported products on the internal market.[5]

The phrase was similarly given a broad meaning in the GATS context. In *EC—Bananas*,[6] the panel held that the ordinary meaning of the term "affecting," in Article I:1 of GATS, did not convey any notion of limiting the scope of the GATS to certain types of measures or to a certain regulatory domain. Rather, the panel decided that Article I:1 refers to measures *in terms of their effect*, which means they could be of any type or relate to any domain of regulation. Since the GATS provisions make no distinc-

---

[2] *Ibid.*, para. 5.4–5.6.

[3] Panel report on *EEC—Regulation on Imports of Parts and Components* (L/6657, adopted on 16 May 1990, BISD 37S/132) para. 5.20–5.21.

[4] Panel report on *United States—Section 337 of the Tariff Act of 1930* (BISD 36S/345, adopted 7 November 1989), para. 5.10.

[5] *Ibid.*, para. 12.

[6] Panel report on *EC—Regime for the Importation, Sale and Distribution of Bananas* (WT/D527/R, adopted on 25 September 1997).

tion between measures which directly govern or regulate services and measures that otherwise affect trade in services, the scope of the GATS and that of GATT were not be considered mutually exclusive. According to the panel, if the drafters of the GATS had intended to impose such a serious limitation on its scope, they would have provided for the limitation explicitly in the text of the GATS itself or in the provisions of the Agreement Establishing the World Trade Organization.[7]

To sum up, Panels and the Appellate Body, both under GATT and GATS, have fended off any attempts to read restrictions into the categories of governmental action capable of infringing the National Treatment obligation. As explicitly stated in the *EC—Bananas* panel report with respect to GATS, the scope of the measures caught by the National Treatment provisions is defined in terms of the regulation's *effects*.

3. The Standard: "Less favourable treatment"

The *locus classicus* in GATT jurisprudence providing the most authoritative interpretation of what constitutes less favourable treatment under Article III:4 is, undoubtedly, the panel report in *United States—Section 337 of the Tariff Act of 1930*.[8] The panel stated that the words "treatment no less favourable" in paragraph 4 call for *effective equality of opportunities for imported products* in respect of the application of laws, regulations and requirements affecting the internal sale, offering for sale, purchase, transportation, distribution or use of products. On the one hand, contracting parties may apply to imported products different formal legal requirements if doing so would accord imported products more favourable treatment. On the other hand, there may be cases where application of formally identical legal provisions would in practice accord less favourable treatment to imported products and a contracting party might thus have to apply different legal provisions to imported products to ensure that the treatment accorded them is in fact no less favourable. Given that the underlying objective is to guarantee equality of treatment, it is incumbent on the contracting party applying differential treatment to show that, in spite of such differences, the no less favourable treatment standard of Article III is met.[9] This ruling stands for the view that National Treatment does not only outlaw formal *de jure* discrimination, but also material *de facto* discrimination. Accordingly,

---

[7] *Ibid.*, paras. 7.283–7.284. These findings of the Panel were upheld in their entirety by the Appellate Body: Appellate Body report on *EC—Regime for the Importation, Sale and Distribution of Bananas* (WT/DS27/AB/R, adopted 25 September 1997) paras. 217–222. See also panel report on *Canada—Certain Measures Concerning Periodicals* (WT/DS31/R, adopted 30 July 1997), paras. 5.13–5.19.

[8] Adopted 7 November 1989, 36S/345.

[9] *Ibid.*, para. 5.11.

National Treatment is an open-ended discipline, which may go as far as imposing a *facere* obligation on Members, i.e. an obligation not simply to accord identical treatment to domestic and foreign products/services, but to differentiate—adapt—domestic regulation if such differentiation is necessary to provide no less favourable treatment to foreign products/services. This approach was codified *explicitis verbis* in Article XVII, paragraphs 2 and 3, and read into GATS Article II, by the *EC—Bananas* panel and Appellate Body reports.[10]

The panel also rejected the view that a complainant had to show the *actual* impact which a measure had on imported products, since a law, regulation or requirement could then only be challenged in GATT after the event as a means of rectifying less favourable treatment of imported products rather than as a means of forestalling it. The panel noted that this approach is in accordance with previous practice of the Contracting Parties in applying Article III, which has been to base their decisions on the distinctions made by the laws, regulations or requirements themselves and on their potential impact, rather than on the actual consequences for specific imported products.[11]

The Appellate Body report on *Korea—Beef*[12] recently emphasised that less favourable treatment can not simply be *assumed* by a panel on the basis that domestic regulation makes a *de jure* distinction in its treatment of imports and domestic production. The panel had stated:

> Any regulatory distinction that is based exclusively on criteria relating to the nationality or the origin of the products is incompatible with Article III [. . .].[13]

The Appellate Body firmly rejected this reasoning:

> Article III:4 requires only that a measure accord treatment to imported products that is "no less favourable" than that accorded to like domestic products. A measure that provides treatment to imported products that is *different* from that accorded to like domestic products is not necessarily inconsistent with Article III:4, as long as the treatment provided by the measure is "no less favourable". According "treatment no less favourable" means, as we have previously said, according *conditions of competition* no less favourable to the imported product than to the like domestic product. [. . .] This interpretation,

---

[10] Although the Panel and the Appellate Body agreed on the outcome, they had based this view on different arguments. Whereas the panel had read *de facto* discrimination into GATS Art. II by reference to paras. 2 and 3 of GATS Art. XVII (Panel Report, para. 7.301), the Appellate Body ruled that "the Panel would have been on safer ground had it compared the MFN obligation in Art. II of the GATS with the MFN and MFN-type obligations in the GATT 1994," which extended to cases of *de facto* discrimination (Appellate Body Report, paras. 231–232).

[11] *Ibid.*, para. 5.13.

[12] Appellate Body report on *Korea—Measures Affecting Imports of Fresh, Chilled, and Frozen Beef* (WT/DS161/AB/R, WT/DS169/AB/R, adopted 10 January 2001).

[13] Panel report on *Korea—Measures Affecting Imports of Fresh, Chilled, and Frozen Beef* (WT/DS161/R, WT/DS169/R, adopted 10 January 2001), para. 627 (footnotes omitted).

which focuses on the *conditions of competition* between imported and domestic like products, implies that a measure according formally *different* treatment to imported products does not *per se*, that is, necessarily, violate Article III:4. [. . .] A formal difference in treatment between imported and like domestic products is thus neither necessary, nor sufficient, to show a violation of Article III:4. Whether or not imported products are treated "less favourably" than like domestic products should be assessed instead by examining whether a measure modifies the *conditions of competition* in the relevant market to the detriment of imported products.[14]

4. The Basis of Comparison: "Likeness"

The definition of likeness has proven to be one of the thorniest issues GATT/WTO panels have had to deal with in the past,[15] in particular in the context of Article III. The debate until now has mainly crystallised two schools of thought. On the one hand, there are those who posit that the likeness of two products should be determined solely on the basis of factors such as their physical similarity, tariff classification, consumer preferences, and end uses. On the other side of the spectrum are the proponents of the so-called aims-and-effects test, who take the view that a determination of likeness should take into account the regulatory objectives of the measure at hand.[16] The latter school had gained momentum during the early nineties, when some GATT panel reports had clearly articulated this test. As soon as it had the opportunity, however, the Appellate Body reversed this case law and appeared to fend off any new attempts to introduce aims and effect in the interpretation of likeness, including in the context of GATS. More recently, the Appellate Body seems to have chosen yet another track, engaging in the assessment of the relative importance of the purported policy objective as such, and allowing risk considerations to be determinative of a discrimination analysis, through the likeness criterion. Below we will only focus on those "milestone" rulings marking the debate.

[14] Appellate Body report, *supra*, paras. 135–137.

[15] A thorough survey of the likeness concept in the various provisions of the covered agreements where the term is used, can be found in Won Mog Choi, *Progressive Interpretation of The Concepts of "Like" And "Directly Competitive Or Substitutable" Products in the GATT/WTO Agreement : The Likeness—Substitutability Problem Of Goods*, unpublished S.J.D. Dissertation, 2001, Georgetown University Law Center (on file with the author). See also Rex Zedalis, "A Theory of the GATT "Like" Product Common Language Cases", 27 *Vanderbilt Journal of Transnational Law* (1994) 33.

[16] A critical overview of the debate can be found in Robert Hudec, "GATT/WTO Constraints on Domestic Regulation: Requiem for an 'Aims and Effects' Test", 32 *The International Lawyer* (1998) 623.

(a) Like Products and Its Interpretation in the Light of the Phrase "So As To Afford Protection"

Traditionally, GATT panels have examined the likeness issue on a case-by-case basis, with reference to four factors: (1) the products' end-uses in a given market; (2) consumers' tastes and habits, which change from country to country; (3) the products' properties, nature and quality; and (4) the products' tariff classification.[17] These criteria were originally inspired on a 1970 report of the Working Party on Border Tax Adjustments.[18]

A different approach was chosen in *United States—Measures Affecting Alcoholic and Malt Beverages*.[19] The panel considered in its report that the like product determination under Article III:2 should also have regard to the purpose of the Article, which is to ensure, as emphasised in Article III:1, "that internal taxes and other internal charges, and laws, regulations and requirements affecting the internal sale, etc. should not be applied to imported or domestic products so as to afford protection to domestic production." It was inferred from this phrase that the purpose of Article III is not to prevent contracting parties from using their fiscal and regulatory powers for purposes other than to afford protection to domestic production by differentiating between different product categories for policy purposes unrelated to the protection of domestic production. The panel considered that this limited purpose of Article III had to be taken into account in interpreting the term "like products" in this provision. Consequently, in determining whether two products subject to different treatment are like products, it would be necessary to consider whether such product differentiation is being made "so as to afford protection to domestic production." This paragraph of the panel report laid the basis for the "aims-and-effects" test.[20]

This approach was elaborated upon in the—unadopted—panel report in *United States—Taxes on Automobiles* ("Gas Guzzler" case).[21] In the panel's view, the practical interpretative issue under paragraphs 2 and 4 of Article III was: which differences between products may form the basis of regulatory distinctions by governments that accord less favourable

---

[17] See, for instance, the working party or panel reports on *The Australian Subsidy on Ammonium Sulphate* (GATT/CP.4/39, adopted 3 April 1950, BISD II/188); *Spain—Tariff Treatment of Unroasted Coffee* (L/5135, adopted 11 June 1981, BISD 28S/102); *United States—Taxes on Petroleum and Certain Imported Substances* (L/6175, adopted 17 June 1987, BISD 34S/136); *Japan—Customs Duties, Taxes and Labelling Practices on Imported Wines and Alcoholic Beverages* (L/6216, adopted 10 November 1987, BISD 34S/83); *EEC—Measures on Animal Feed Proteins* (L/6627, adopted 25 January 1990, BISD 37S/86).

[18] L/3464, adopted 2 December 1970, BISD 18S/97, 102.

[19] Panel report on *US—Measures affecting Alcoholic and Malt Beverages* (DS23, adopted 19 June 1992, 39S/206).

[20] *Ibid.*, para. 5.25.

[21] DS31/R, not adopted, reprinted in 33 ILM 1397.

treatment to imported products?[22] The panel considered that paragraphs 2 and 4 of Article III had to be read in the light of Article III:1, and that Article III serves only to prohibit regulatory distinctions between products applied so as to afford protection to domestic production. Non-protectionist government policies might, however, require regulatory distinctions that were not based on the product's end use, its physical characteristics, etc. Noting that a primary purpose of the GATT was to lower barriers to trade between markets, and not to harmonise the regulatory treatment of products within them, the panel considered that Article III could not be interpreted as prohibiting government policy options, based on products, that were not taken so as to afford protection to domestic production. In the panel's view, the determination of the relevant features common to the domestic and imported products had to include an examination of the *aim and effect* of the particular tax measure.[23]

Applying this theory to the facts at hand, the panel considered that the contested US excise tax on luxury cars did not violate Article III:2, because the technology to manufacture high fuel economy automobiles—above the regulatory threshold—was not *inherent* to the United States, nor were low fuel economy automobiles *inherently* of foreign origin. Thus, according to the panel, the fact that EC automobiles bore most of the burden of the tax did not mean that the measure had the effect of affording protection to United States production. The EC took vehemently objection against the panel report, as a result of which it was never adopted by the Contracting Parties.[24]

The success of the aims-and-effects test, however, would be short-lived. It was resolutely rejected by the first panel established under the WTO DSU that had the opportunity to rule explicitly on the issue with respect to Article III:2. In *Japan—Taxes on Alcoholic Beverages,*[25] the panel proceeded to an analysis of how the legal obligations imposed by Article III:2, first sentence, should be interpreted. The panel rejected the aims-and-effects variants which had been proffered by the US and Japan in their submissions, considering that such a test is not consistent with the wording of Article III:2, first sentence. The panel made various objections: the basis of the aim-and-effect test is found in the words "so as to afford protection" contained in Article III:1 and Article III:2, first sentence, contains no reference to those words; the adoption of the aim-and-effect test would have important repercussions on the burden of proof imposed on the complainant; in case of a multiplicity of aims, it

---

[22] *Ibid.*, para. 5.5.
[23] *Ibid.*, para. 5.8.
[24] *Ibid.*, para. 5.14.
[25] Panel report on *Japan—Taxes on Alcoholic Beverages* (WT/DS8/R, adopted 1 November 1996).

would be a difficult exercise to determine which aim or aims should be determinative for applying the aim-and-effect test; access to the complete legislative history could be difficult or even impossible for a complaining party to obtain;[26] the list of exceptions contained in Article XX of GATT 1994 could become redundant or useless because the aim-and-effect test does not contain a definitive list of grounds justifying departure from the obligations that are otherwise incorporated in Article III.[27] In sum, the panel concluded that for reasons relating to the wording of Article III as well as its context, the aim-and-effect test proposed by Japan and the United States should be rejected.[28]

The panel Report was appealed. The Appellate Body upheld the findings of the panel as regards likeness, although it did find fault with some of the panel's reasoning. It considered that Article III:1 articulated a general principle that internal measures should not be applied so as to afford protection to domestic production, and that this general principle informed the rest of Article III. In the view of the Appellate Body, the purpose of Article III:1 is to establish this general principle as a guide to understanding and interpreting the specific obligations contained in Article III:2 and in the other paragraphs of Article III, while respecting, and not diminishing in any way, the meaning of the words actually used in the texts of those other paragraphs:[29]

—Article III:1 informed Article III:2, *first sentence*, by establishing that if imported products were taxed in excess of like domestic products, then that tax measure was inconsistent with Article III. There is no specific invocation in this first sentence of the general principle in Article III:1 that admonishes Members of the WTO not to apply measures "so as to afford protection." In the view of the Appellate Body, this omission meant that the presence of a "protective application" need not be established separately from the specific requirements that are included in the first sentence in order to show that a tax measure is inconsistent with the general principle set out in the first sentence. However, this did not mean that the general principle of Article III:1 does not apply to this sentence. To the contrary, the Appellate Body considered that the first sentence of Article III:2 was, in effect, an application of this general principle.[30]

---

[26] Panel report on *Japan—Taxes on Alcoholic Beverages* (WT/DS8/R, adopted 1 November 1996) para. 4.16.

[27] *Ibid.*, para. 6.17. See also para. 8.130 of the panel report on *European Communities—Measures Affecting Asbestos and Asbestos-Containing Products* (WT/DS135/R, adopted 5 April 2001): "We consider that introducing a criterion on the risk of a product into the analysis of likeness within the meaning of Art. III would largely nullify the effect of Art. XX(b)."

[28] *Ibid.*

[29] Appellate Body report on *Japan—Taxes on Alcoholic Beverages* (WT/DS8/R, adopted 1 November 1996), p. 18.

[30] *Ibid.*, p. 19.

—As regards the *second* sentence of Article III:2—which does explicitly refer to Article III:1—the Appellate Body considered that the phrase "so as to afford protection" in Article III:1 is not an issue of *intent*. It was not necessary for a panel to sort through the many reasons legislators and regulators often have for what they do and weigh the relative significance of those reasons to establish legislative or regulatory intent. According to the Appellate Body, this was an issue of how the measure in question is *applied*.[31] An examination of whether dissimilar taxation has been applied so as to afford protection requires "a comprehensive and objective analysis of the structure and application of the measure in question" on domestic as compared to imported products. It considered that the protective application of a measure can most often be discerned from *the design, the architecture, and the revealing structure of a measure*.[32]

The Appellate Body conceded that the determination by a panel of "likeness" would always involve an unavoidable element of individual, discretionary judgement, and that no one approach to exercising judgement will be appropriate for all cases. There could be no one precise and absolute definition of what is "like." The concept of "likeness" was, in its view, a relative one that evokes the image of an accordion.

This "protective application" theory espoused by the Appellate Body under the second sentence of Article III:2 was neatly applied by the panel in *Korea—Taxes on Alcoholic Beverages*[33] and confirmed by the Appellate Body on appeal.[34] The Appellate Body appeared to have slightly retreated from this position, however, in its report on *Canada—Certain Measures concerning Periodicals*.[35] There, in support of its conclusive finding as regards the "protective application" of the measures at issue, the Appellate Body relied on—and quoted extensively verbatim from—public statements by the defendant's government officials indicating a protective aim,[36] hence clearly "sort[ing] through the many reasons legislators and regulators often have for what they do and weigh[ing] the relative significance of those reasons to establish legislative or regulatory intent."

Provisionally (but certainly not definitively) the last case in which a panel was called upon to interpret Article III:2 is *Chile—Taxes on Alcoholic*

---

[31] *Ibid.*, p. 27.

[32] *Ibid.*, p. 28–29.

[33] Panel report on *Korea—Taxes on Alcoholic Beverages* (WT/DS75/R, adopted 17 February 1999), paras. 10.101–10.102.

[34] Appellate Body report on *Korea—Taxes on Alcoholic Beverages* (WT/DS75/AB/R, adopted 17 February 1999), paras. 146–150.

[35] Appellate Body report on *Canada—Certain Measures concerning Periodicals* (WT/DS31/AB/R, adopted 30 July 1997).

[36] *Ibid.*, p. 31.

Beverages.[37] The panel was requested to rule on the WTO-consistency of a Chilean Special Sales Tax on Spirits ("the Sales Tax"). The Sales Tax provided a transitional tax system for distilled spirits which was applicable until 1 December 2000, and a revised tax system (the "New Chilean System") which was to be applied from 1 December 2000. The New Chilean System taxed all spirits on the basis of their alcohol content and price. Spirits with an alcohol content of 35° or less were taxed at a rate of 27 per cent *ad valorem*. From a rate of 27 per cent *ad valorem*, the tax rate increased in increments of 4 percentage points per additional degree of alcohol, until a maximum rate of 47 per cent *ad valorem* is reached for all spirits over 39°. The panel found that roughly 75 per cent of the total volume of domestically produced spirits would be taxed at 27 per cent *ad valorem*, while over 95 per cent of the total volume of imported spirits would be taxed at 47 per cent *ad valorem*. The panel considered claims made by the European Communities that the measure at issue is inconsistent with Article III:2, second sentence, of GATT because it accords preferential tax treatment to pisco, a distilled alcoholic beverage produced in Chile, thereby affording "protection" to domestic production in relation to certain imported alcoholic beverages. The panel reached the conclusion that "the domestic distilled alcoholic beverages produced in Chile, including pisco, and the imported products presently identified by HS classification 2208, are directly competitive or substitutable products," that the "Transitional System and [the] New Chilean System provide for dissimilar taxation of the imports in an amount that is greater than *de minimis* levels," and, finally, that the dissimilar taxation in both systems was "applied in a manner so as to afford protection to Chile's domestic production."[38] As a result, the panel concluded that there was nullification or impairment of the benefits accruing to the complainant under GATT and recommended that the DSB request Chile to bring its taxes on distilled alcoholic beverages into conformity with its obligations under GATT.

The panel report is of interest in two respects. First, the panel noted the reliance by the Appellate Body in *Canada—Certain Measures concerning Periodicals* on legislative intent and considered that "[t]o a certain extent, this may appear as a change by the Appellate Body in their approach to this part of the analysis of Article III:2, second sentence."[39] The panel considered that the stated objectives by the government of the Member concerned may be relevant in evaluating the design of a measure.[40] Chile appealed against the panel Report, focusing its challenge on

[37] Panel report on *Chile—Taxes on Alcoholic Beverages* (WT/DS87/R, adopted 12 January 2000).

[38] *Ibid.*, para. 7.159.

[39] *Ibid.*, para. 7.118.

[40] *Ibid.*, para. 7.120.

the interpretation and application of Article III:1. The Appellate Body upheld the panel's finding, reiterating its position that:

> The *subjective* intentions inhabiting the minds of individual legislators or regulators do not bear upon the inquiry, if only because they are not accessible to treaty interpreters. It does not follow, however, that the statutory purposes or objectives—that is, the purpose or objectives of a Member's legislature and government as a whole—to the extent that they are given *objective* expression in the statute itself, are not pertinent. (original emphasis)[41]

Second, and more importantly, in a crucial passage of the report, which seems to have gone unnoticed by most scholars and practitioners alike, the panel explained how it arrived at its conclusion that the dissimilar taxation was applied in a manner "so as to afford protection":

> In [the Panel's] view, the failure of a measure to conform to its stated objectives may be indicative of certain aspects of its design, structure and architecture. That is, while [the Panel] will not examine the stated objective itself to determine its legitimacy, it is a relevant inquiry to examine the *relationship* between the stated objective and the measure in question. If a rational relationship between the stated objective and the measure is lacking, this may provide evidence of protective application, which we will take into consideration along with other factors.[42]

The panel then applied this test to the concrete tax measures under examination, finding that either "there is no rational reason why such a structure as devised by Chile is *necessary* for this purpose," or "the New Chilean System *does not achieve* [the goal of eliminating type distinctions]," or "[the measure] *may achieve* such a result, although the evidence seems to be more persuasive to the contrary" (emphasis added).[43]

The Chilean government challenged this finding of the panel in its appeal before the Appellate Body, asserting that:

> The Panel erred in finding that the stated objectives of the measure were "inconsistent" with the measure. While perhaps not fully successful in achieving the objectives, the measure is not inconsistent with its goals. *Such a finding constitutes an indirect evaluation by the Panel of the "efficiency" of the policies of WTO Members.* This is inappropriate. A WTO Member has the right to choose between different tax systems and the mere fact that one system may "inconvenience" imports more than another system does not render it inconsistent with WTO law.[44]

---

[41] Appellate Body Report on *Chile—Taxes on Alcoholic Beverages* (WT/DS87/AB/R, adopted 12 January 2000), para. 62.

[42] Panel report, *supra* n. 38, para. 7.148. Original emphasis.

[43] *Ibid.*, paras. 7.149–7.153.

[44] Appellate Body Report, *supra* n. 41, para. 14. Emphasis added.

The Appellate Body replied to the Chilean concern by stating:

> We agree with Chile that it would be inappropriate, under Article III:2, second sentence, of the GATT 1994, to examine whether the tax measure is *necessary* for achieving its stated objectives or purposes. The panel did use the word "necessary" in this part of its reasoning. Nevertheless, we do not read the Panel report as showing that the Panel did, in fact, conduct an examination of whether the measure is necessary to achieve its stated objectives. *It appears to us that the panel did no more than try to relate the observable structural features of the measure with its declared purposes, a task that is unavoidable in appraising the application of the measure as protective or not of domestic production.*[45]

The *Chile—Taxes* opinions raise the question as to whether the panel conducted, and the Appellate Body condoned, an in-depth *necessity* test as regards domestic regulation under GATT Article III:2, second sentence, despite their formally denying doing so. Put another way, did the panel and the Appellate Body hold that the discriminatory character of a domestic regulation is revealed under GATT Article III:2, second sentence, by the lack of a "necessary" relationship between the measure and the purported policy goal? Below, we will argue that they did indeed do so.

These cases all dealt with Article III:2 (or, by reference, to Article III:1). With regard to Article III:4, the panel in *United States—Standards for Reformulated and Conventional Gasoline*, a pre-*Japan—Alcoholic Beverages* case, stated, in reply to the US' suggestion of an aims-and-effects test under Article III:4:

> Apart from being contrary to the ordinary meaning of the terms of Article III:4, any interpretation of Article III:4 in this manner would mean that the treatment of imported and domestic goods concerned could no longer be assured on the objective basis of their likeness as products. Rather, imported goods would be exposed to a highly subjective and variable treatment according to extraneous factors. This would thereby create great instability and uncertainty in the conditions of competition as between domestic and imported goods in a manner fundamentally inconsistent with the object and purpose of Article III.[47]

The panel in *EC—Bananas*, however, had to rule on the issue after the *Japan—Alcoholic Beverages* decision was issued, and considered it appropriate, in reference to the Appellate Body's decision in *Japan—Alcoholic Beverages*, to base its ruling on the Appellate Body's consideration that the protective application of a measure can most often be discerned from the design, the architecture, and the revealing structure of the measure.[48] On appeal, however, the Appellate Body sharply

---

[45] *Ibid.*, para. 72. Original emphasis in first sentence, added in second sentence.

[47] Panel report on *United States—Standards for Reformulated and Conventional Gasoline* (WT/DS32/R, adopted 20 May 1996), para. 6.39.

[48] Panel report on *EC—Regime for the Importation, Sale and Distribution of Bananas*, *supra* n. 6, para. 7.181.

rejected this finding. It stated that the panel had misinterpreted its decision in *Japan—Alcoholic Beverages*. Since Article III:4, like Article III:2, first sentence, does not specifically refer to Article III:1, a determination of whether there has been a violation of Article III:4 does not require a separate consideration of whether a measure "affords protection to domestic production."[49] The panel diligently followed this ruling in its report on *Canada—Autos*.[50] In its report on *EC—Asbestos*,[51] the panel did the same as regards Article III:4,[52] but, interestingly, proposed to apply the protective application theory to the term "disguised restriction" in the chapeau of Article XX.[53]

The Appellate Body report on *EC—Asbestos* is the most comprehensive and recent statement of the law regarding likeness in Article III:4.[54] The following considerations by the Appellate Body should be highlighted:

First, the Appellate Body defined the scope of likeness in paragraph 4 using paragraphs 1 and 2 as context. The Appellate Body noted that the "general principle" articulated in Article III:1 is expressed in Article III:4, not through two distinct obligations, as in the two sentences in Article III:2, but instead through a single obligation that applies solely to "like products". Therefore, given the textual difference between Articles III:2 and III:4, the "accordion" of "likeness" stretches in a different way in Article III:4. The Appellate Body considered that it would be incongruous if, due to a significant difference in the product scope of paragraphs 2 and 4 of Article III, Members were prevented from using one form of regulation—for instance, fiscal—to protect domestic production of certain products, but were able to use another form of regulation—for instance, non-fiscal—to achieve those ends. The Appellate Body therefore concluded that the scope of "like" in Article III:4 is broader than the scope of "like" in Article III:2, first sentence, and that the product scope of Article III:4, although broader than the *first* sentence of Article III:2, is certainly *not* broader than the *combined* product scope of the *two* sentences of Article III:2 of the GATT 1994.[55]

---

[49] Appellate Body Report on *EC—Regime for the Importation, Sale and Distribution of Bananas, supra* n. 7, para. 216.

[50] Panel report on *Canada—Certain Measures Affecting the Automotive Industry* (WT/DS139/R, adopted 19 June 2000), para. 10.78.

[51] Panel report on *European Communities—Measures Affecting Asbestos and Asbestos-Containing Products, supra* n. 27.

[52] *Ibid.*, para. 8.112 and following.

[53] *Ibid.*, para. 8.236.

[54] Appellate Body report on *European Communities—Measures Affecting Asbestos and Asbestos-Containing Products* (WT/DS135/AB/R, adopted 5 April 2001).

[55] *Ibid.*, paras. 93–99. *Cf.* the panel report on *Japan—Taxes on Alcoholic Beverages, supra* n. 25, where the Panel had "noted the discrepancy between Art. III:2, on the one hand, and Art. III:4, on the other: while the former referred to Art. III:1 and to like as well as to directly competitive or substitutable products [...], the latter referred only to like products. If the coverage of Art. III:2 is identical to that of Art. III:4, a different interpretation of the term "like product" would be called for in the two paragraphs. Otherwise, if the term "like product"

Second, in the Appellate Body's view, having adopted an approach based on the four criteria set forth in *Border Tax Adjustments*, a panel should examine the evidence relating to *each* of those four criteria and, then, weigh *all* of that evidence, along with any other relevant evidence, in making an *overall* determination of whether the products at issue could be characterised as "like". The panel in this case erred by basing its findings on its assessment on the evidence relating to only one of the four criteria.[56]

Third, reversing the panel's findings in this respect, the Appellate Body was of the view that evidence relating to the health risks associated with a product may be pertinent in an examination of "likeness" under Article III:4 of the GATT 1994. According to the Appellate Body, however, the evidence relating to the health risks associated with chrysotile asbestos fibres need not be examined under a *separate* criterion, because this evidence can be evaluated under the existing criteria of physical properties and of consumers' tastes and habits.[57] In this case, the Appellate Body considered that the carcinogenicity, or toxicity, constitutes a defining aspect of the physical properties of chrysotile asbestos fibres.[58] It was also persuaded that evidence relating to consumers' tastes and habits would establish that the health risks associated with chrysotile asbestos fibres influence consumers' behaviour with respect to the different fibres at issue. The Appellate Body highlighted that consumers' tastes and habits regarding fibres, even in the case of commercial parties, such as manufacturers, are very likely to be shaped by the health risks associated with a product which is known to be highly carcinogenic.[59]

Fourth, the Appellate Body did not accept Canada's contention that, in markets where normal conditions of competition have been disturbed by regulatory or fiscal barriers, consumers' tastes and habits cease to be relevant. In such situations, a Member may submit evidence of latent, or suppressed, consumer demand in that market, or it may submit evidence of substitutability from some relevant third market.[60]

Fifth, the Appellate Body did not agree with the panel that considering evidence relating to the health risks associated with a product, under Article III:4, nullifies the effect of Article XX(b) of the GATT 1994. The fact that an interpretation of Article III:4, under those rules, implies a less frequent recourse to Article XX(b) does not deprive the exception in

were to be interpreted in an identical way in both instances, the scope of the two paragraphs would be different." *Ibid.*, para. 6.20.

[56] Appellate Body report on *European Communities—Measures Affecting Asbestos and Asbestos-Containing Products, supra* n. 54, para. 109.

[57] *Ibid.*, para. 113.

[58] *Ibid.*, para. 114.

[59] *Ibid.*, para. 122.

[60] *Ibid.*, para. 123.

Article XX(b) of *effet utile*. Article XX(b) would only be deprived of *effet utile* if that provision could not serve to allow a Member to "adopt and enforce" measures "necessary to protect human . . . life or health". Evaluating evidence relating to the health risks arising from the physical properties of a product does not prevent a measure which is inconsistent with Article III:4 from being justified under Article XX(b).[61]

Finally, in the Appellate Body's view, in cases where the evidence relating to physical properties establishes that the products at issue are physically quite different, in order to overcome this indication that products are *not* "like", a higher burden is placed on complaining Members to establish that, despite the pronounced physical differences, there is a competitive relationship between the products such that *all* of the evidence, taken together, demonstrates that the products are "like" under Article III:4 of the GATT 1994.[62]

(b) Like Services and Service Suppliers

The first instance where a panel and the Appellate Body were called upon to interpret likeness in GATS Article XVII was *EC—Bananas*.[63] The panel dealt with the matter in a remarkably summary fashion:

> [I]n our view, *the nature and the characteristics* of wholesale transactions as such, as well as of each of the different subordinated services mentioned in the headnote to section 6 of the CPC, are "like" when supplied in connection with wholesale services, irrespective of whether these services are supplied with respect to bananas of EC and traditional ACP origin, on the one hand, or with respect to bananas of third-country or non-traditional ACP origin, on the other. Indeed, it seems that each of the different service activities taken individually is virtually the same and can only be distinguished by referring to the origin of the bananas in respect of which the service activity is being performed. Similarly, in our view, *to the extent that entities provide these like services, they are like service suppliers.*[64]

On appeal, the EC had argued that the EC licensing system for bananas was not discriminatory under Articles II and XVII of the GATS, because the various aspects of the system, including the operator category rules, the activity function rules and the special hurricane licence rules, "pursue entirely legitimate policies" and "are not inherently discriminatory in design or effect." The EC thus basically posited that the panel should have applied the aims-and-effects test, which the EC had traditionally rejected.[65]

[61] *Ibid.*, para. 125.
[62] *Ibid.*, para. 118.
[63] Panel report on *EC—Regime for the Importation, Sale and Distribution of Bananas, supra* n. 6.
[64] *Ibid.*, para. 7.322.
[65] Appellate Body Report on *EC—Regime for the Importation, Sale and Distribution of Bananas, supra* n. 7, para. 57.

The Appellate Body did not accept the argument. It saw no specific authority either in Article II or in Article XVII of the GATS for the proposition that the "aims and effects" of a measure are in any way relevant in determining whether that measure is inconsistent with those provisions. It pointed out that in the GATT context, the "aims and effects" theory had its origins in the phrase "so as to afford protection to domestic production," and that there is no comparable provision in the GATS.[66]

The interpretation of likeness of service suppliers espoused in the *EC—Bananas* report was subsequently endorsed by the panel in *Canada—Autos*, although the panel here added that this interpretation constitutes the right likeness standard "for the purpose of this case", apparently leaving the door open to alternative criteria in future cases.

B. EXISTING LIMITATIONS ON THE SCOPE OF *DE FACTO* DISCRIMINATION:
LEGITIMATE OBJECTIVES AND LEAST RESTRICTIVE MEANS UNDER GATT AND GATS

When a domestic regulation has been found to be discriminatory, be it *de jure* or *de facto*, and hence in breach of GATT Article III:4 or GATS Article XVII, it can still be saved under the well-known provisions of GATT Article XX or GATS Article XIV. Put another way, under both GATT and GATS, the legitimacy of the regulatory objective can only be considered after a violation of National Treatment has been found. Apart from enumerating, apparently in an exhaustive manner,[67] the regulatory goals capable of being saved, both provisions also qualify the connection which need to be demonstrated between the regulation and the regulatory objective.

As for GATT Article XX, the Appellate Body has interpreted this provision as laying down a two-tiered justification test. First, "provisional justification" by reason of characterisation of the measure under one of the paragraphs of Article XX. Second, "further appraisal" of the measure under the introductory clauses of Article XX, the Chapeau.[68] As regards the first step, it was noted earlier that the language qualifying the connection between regulation and goal varies widely: it must either be

---

[66] *Ibid.*, para. 241.

[67] Although para. (d) arguably allows for the inclusion of other legitimate policy objectives, provided the conditions stipulated in that provision have been met.

[68] Appellate Body report on *United States—Standards for Reformulated and Conventional Gasoline*, Appellate Body Report (WT/DS2/AB/R, adopted 20 May 1996), p. 21; confirmed in the Appellate Body report on *United States—Import Prohibition of Certain Shrimp and Shrimp Products* (WT/DS58/AB/R, adopted 6 November 1998), paras. 8–9.

"necessary,"[69] "relating to,"[70] "in pursuance of,"[71] "essential,"[72] "for the protection of,"[73] or involving."[74] The Appellate Body has inferred from this that the WTO Members must have intended to impart a different meaning to each of these connectors.[75] Of the latter, only the connectors "necessary" and "relating to" have been interpreted by panels and/or Appellate Body on several occasions, in particular in the context of measures purported to pursue an environmental or public health policy goal. "Relating to," on the one hand, has traditionally been interpreted as meaning "primarily aimed at."[76] "Necessary", on the other hand, has been interpreted in the context of Article XX(d) by the panel in the *Section 337* case as a least restrictive means test:

> a contracting party cannot justify a measure inconsistent with another GATT provision as "necessary" in terms of Article XX(d) if an alternative measure which it could reasonably be expected to employ and which is not inconsistent with other GATT provisions is available to it. By the same token, in cases where a measure consistent with other GATT provisions is not reasonably available, a contracting party is bound to use, among the measures reasonably available to it, that which entails the least degree of inconsistency with other GATT provisions.[77]

The same reasoning was subsequently adopted by the *Thai Cigarette* panel in examining a measure under Article XX(b),[78] and confirmed in *US—Gasoline*.[79] The recent Appellate Body report in *Korea—Beef*,[80] however, has added some important observations s regards the interpretation of this necessity test.[81] The Appellate Body started out by noting that the word "necessary" normally denotes something "that cannot be dispensed with or done without, requisite, essential, needful". [82] It

[69] Paras. (a), (b) and (d).
[70] Paras. (c), (e) and (g).
[71] Para. (h).
[72] Para. (j).
[73] Para. (f).
[74] Para. (i).
[75] Appellate Body report on *United States—Standards for Reformulated and Conventional Gasoline, supra* n. 68, p. 17.
[76] See panel report on *Canada—Measures Affecting Exports of Unprocessed Herring and Salmon* (L/6268, adopted 22 March 1988, BISD 35S/98), para. 4.6; confirmed in panel report on *United States—Standards for Reformulated and Conventional Gasoline, supra* n. 47, para. 6.39.
[77] Panel report on *United States—Section 337 of the Tariff Act of 1930* (L/6439, adopted 7 November 1989, BISD 36S/345), para. 5.26.
[78] Panel report on *Thailand—Restrictions on Importation of and Internal Taxes on Cigarettes* (DS10/R, adopted 7 November 1990, BISD 37S/200), para. 75.
[79] Panel report on *United States—Standards for Reformulated and Conventional Gasoline, supra* n. 47, paras. 6.24–6.25.
[80] Appellate Body report on *Korea—Measures Affecting Imports of Fresh, Chilled and Frozen Beef, supra* n. 12.
[81] *Ibid.*, paras. 160–182.
[82] The Appellate Body drew this definition from *The New Shorter Oxford English Dictionary*, (Clarendon Press, 1993), Vol. II, p. 1895.

also noted, however, that a standard law dictionary cautions that "[t]his word must be considered in the connection in which it is used, as it is a word susceptible of various meanings. [. . .] It is an adjective expressing degrees, and may express mere convenience or that which is indispensable or an absolute physical necessity". [83]

It then submitted that,

> as used in the context of Article XX(d), the reach of the word "necessary" is not limited to that which is "indispensable" or "of absolute necessity" or "inevitable". Measures which are indispensable or of absolute necessity or inevitable to secure compliance certainly fulfil the requirements of Article XX(d). But other measures, too, may fall within the ambit of this exception. As used in Article XX(d), the term "necessary" refers, in our view, to a range of degrees of necessity. At one end of this continuum lies "necessary" understood as "indispensable"; at the other end, is "necessary" taken to mean as "making a contribution to." We consider that a "necessary" measure is, in this continuum, located significantly closer to the pole of "indispensable" than to the opposite pole of simply "making a contribution to.[84]

According to the Appellate Body, in appraising the "necessity" of a measure in these terms, it is useful to bear in mind the context in which "necessary" is found in Article XX(d). The measure at stake has to be "necessary to ensure compliance with laws and regulations . . . , *including* those relating to customs enforcement, the enforcement of [lawful] monopolies . . . , the protection of patents, trade marks and copyrights, and the prevention of deceptive practices". The Appellate Body infers from this that Article XX(d) is susceptible of application in respect of a wide variety of "laws and regulations" to be enforced. In its view, the strictness of the necessity test would be a function of various parameters. Along these lines, it opines that a treaty interpreter assessing a measure claimed to be necessary to secure compliance of a WTO-consistent law or regulation may, in appropriate cases, take into account:

—the relative importance of the common interests or values that the law or regulation to be enforced is intended to protect. *The more vital or important those common interests or values are, the easier it would be to accept as "necessary" a measure designed as an enforcement instrument.*[85]
—the extent to which the measure contributes to the realisation of the end pursued, the securing of compliance with the law or regulation at issue. *The greater the contribution, the more easily a measure might be considered to be "necessary".*[86]

---

[83] The Appellate Body drew this paragraph from *Black's Law Dictionary*, (West Publishing, 1995), p. 1029.

[84] Appellate Body report on *Korea—Measures Affecting Imports of Fresh, Chilled and Frozen Beef, supra* n. 12, para. 161.

[85] *Ibid.*, para. 162.

[86] *Ibid.*, para. 163.

—the extent to which the compliance measure produces restrictive effects on international commerce, that is, in respect of a measure inconsistent with Article III:4, restrictive effects on imported goods. *A measure with a relatively slight impact upon imported products might more easily be considered as "necessary" than a measure with intense or broader restrictive effects.*[87]

In sum, according to the Appellate Body, determination of whether a measure, which is not "indispensable", may nevertheless be "necessary" within the contemplation of Article XX(d), involves in every case a process of weighing and balancing a series of factors "which prominently include" the contribution made by the compliance measure to the enforcement of the law or regulation at issue, the importance of the common interests or values protected by that law or regulation, and the accompanying impact of the law or regulation on imports or exports.[88]

In the Appellate Body's view, the standard described by the panel in *United States—Section 337* encapsulates this weighing and balancing process, since it is comprehended in the determination of whether a WTO-consistent alternative measure which the Member concerned could "reasonably be expected to employ" is available, or whether a less WTO-inconsistent measure is "reasonably available".[89]

In its determination of the reasonable availability of alternatives, the panel had inferred from the absence of any requirement for a dual retail system in related product areas, that reasonable alternatives did indeed exist. In its appeal, Korea had argued that the panel, by drawing such conclusions, had introduced an illegitimate "consistency test" into Article XX(d). For Korea, the proper test for "necessary" under Article XX(d) "[. . .] is to see whether another means exists which is less restrictive than the one used and which can reach the objective sought. Whether such means will be applied *consistently* to other products or not is not a matter of concern for the necessity requirement under Article XX(d)."[90] The Appellate Body, however, approved of the panel's approach. In its view, examining enforcement measures applicable to the same illegal behaviour relating to like, or at least similar, products does not necessarily imply the introduction of a "consistency" requirement into the "necessary" concept of Article XX(d). Examining such enforcement measures may provide useful input in the course of determining whether an alternative measure which could "reasonably be expected" to be utilised, is available or not.[91] The application by a Member of WTO-compatible enforcement measures to the same kind of

[87] *Ibid.*
[88] *Ibid.*, para.164.
[89] *Ibid.*, para. 166.
[90] *Ibid.*, para. 167.
[91] *Ibid.*, para. 170.

illegal behaviour—the passing off of one product for another—for like or at least similar products, provides a suggestive indication that an alternative measure which could "reasonably be expected" to be employed may well be available. The application of such measures for the control of the same illegal behaviour for like, or at least similar, products raises doubts with respect to the objective *necessity* of a different, much stricter, and WTO-inconsistent enforcement measure.[92]

On appeal, Korea had also argued that alternative measures must not only be reasonably available, but must also *guarantee* the level of enforcement sought which, in the case of the dual retail system, is the *elimination* of fraud in the beef retail market. [93] The Appellate Body did not sustain this argument. In its opinion, it is not open to doubt that Members of the WTO have the right to determine for themselves the level of enforcement of their WTO-consistent laws and regulations. However, it thought it "unlikely" that Korea intended to establish a level of protection that *totally eliminates* fraud with respect to the origin of beef (domestic or foreign) sold by retailers, since "the total elimination of fraud would probably require a total ban of imports." Consequently, the Appellate Body assumed that in effect Korea rather intended to *reduce considerably* the number of cases of fraud occurring with respect to the origin of beef sold by retailers.[94]

Finally, the Appellate Body "found it pertinent to observe" that, through its dual retail system, Korea had in effect shifted all, or the great bulk, of the potential costs of enforcement (translated into a drastic reduction of competitive access to consumers) to imported goods and retailers of imported goods, instead of evenly distributing such costs between the domestic and imported products. In contrast, the more conventional, WTO-consistent measures of enforcement did not involve such onerous shifting of enforcement costs which ordinarily are borne by the Member's public purse.[95]

The Appellate Body reiterated this approach to necessity in *EC—Asbestos*, where it stated that the preservation of human life and health constitutes a value which is "both vital and important in the highest degree."[96]

Once a measure has been cleared as being either necessary for or relating to the achievement of an objective, the second step in an Article XX analysis consists of examining whether the measure constitutes

---

[92] Appellate Body report on *Korea—Measures Affecting Imports of Fresh, Chilled and Frozen Beef, supra* n. 12, para. 172.

[93] Paras. 181, 185.

[94] *Ibid.*, paras. 175–178.

[95] *Ibid.*, para. 181.

[96] Appellate Body report on *European Communities—Measures Affecting Asbestos and Asbestos-Containing Products, supra* n. 54, para. 172.

"arbitrary discrimination," "unjustifiable discrimination," or "disguised restriction on international trade" under the Chapeau of Article XX. According to the Appellate Body, these terms should be read side-by-side: they impart meaning to one another. They have to be interpreted in the light of the purpose and object of avoiding abuse or illegitimate use of the exceptions to substantive rules available in Article XX.[97] This test is, according to the Appellate Body, merely an expression of the principle of good faith in international law.[98] It is the task of "locating and marking out a line of equilibrium between the rights of a member to invoke an exception under Article XX and the rights of the other Members under [. . .] the GATT 1994, so that neither of the competing rights will cancel out the other and thereby distort and nullify or impair the balance of rights and obligations constructed by the Members themselves in that Agreements."[99] According to the Appellate Body, it is the way in which a measure is *applied*—not the measure as such—which needs to be examined under the chapeau of GATT Article XX.[100]

The panel in *European Communities—Measures Affecting Asbestos and Asbestos-Containing Products* has recently proposed to use the protective application theory developed by the Appellate Body in relation to GATT Article III:2, second sentence (and rejected in relation to both GATT Article III:4 and GATS Article XVII), to interpret the phrase "disguised restriction" in the chapeau. According to the panel, "[a]lthough this approach was developed in relation to Article III:4 [sic] of the GATT 1994, we see no reason why it should not be applicable in other circumstances where it is necessary to determine whether a measure is being applied for protective purposes."[101]

As for GATS, no panel or Appellate Body has yet had the opportunity to pronounce itself on Article XIV. It suffices to recall that the Chapeau has been drafted in identical terms, and that, with the exception of one paragraph, the connector used is necessity.

---

[97] Appellate Body report on *United States—Standards for Reformulated and Conventional Gasoline, supra* n. 68, p. 24.

[98] Appellate Body report on *United States—Import Prohibition of Certain Shrimp and Shrimp Products, supra* n. 68, para. 48.

[99] *Ibid.*, para. 49.

[100] See Appellate Body reports on *United States—Standards for Reformulated and Conventional Gasoline, supra* n. 68, p. 25; *United States—Import Prohibition of Certain Shrimp and Shrimp Products, supra* n. 68, para. 115; and the panel report on *European Communities—Measures Affecting Asbestos and Asbestos-Containing Products, supra* n. 68, para. 8.226.

[101] Footnote 199 of the Panel report on *European Communities—Measures Affecting Asbestos and Asbestos-Containing Products, supra* n. 27. Not addressed on appeal.

C. NATIONAL TREATMENT AND NON-VIOLATION

The remedy of non-violation complaints under GATT Article XXIII:2(b)[102] has been a continuous source of polemics among scholars.[103] Despite criticism as regards the applicability of its underlying premises, the non-violation remedy was maintained during the Uruguay Round under the GATT, its rationale extended to GATS[104] and—albeit subject to a five-year moratorium—to TRIPS,[105] and its specific procedural rules codified in the DSU.[106] The treaty drafters' rationale for having a non-violation remedy in the GATT was succinctly formulated in the panel report on *EEC—Payments and Subsidies Paid to Processors and Producers of Oilseeds and Related Animal-Feed Proteins*:

> The Panel noted that these provisions, as conceived by the drafters and applied by the contracting parties, serve mainly to protect the value of tariff concessions. The idea underlying [the provisions of Article XXIII:3(b)] is that that the improved competitive opportunities that can legitimately be expected from a tariff concession can be frustrated not only by measures proscribed by the General Agreement but also by measures consistent with that Agreement. In order to encourage contracting parties to make tariff concessions they must therefore be given a right of redress when a reciprocal concession is impaired

---

[102] See, generally, World Trade Organization, *Non-Violation Complaints under Article XXIII:2*, MTN.GNG/NG13/W/31.

[103] See, for instance, Sung-Joon Cho, "GATT Non-Violation Issues in the WTO Framework: Are they the Achilles' Heel of the Dispute Settlement Process?", 39 *Harvard International Law Review* (1998) 311; Thomas Cottier and Kristina Nadakavukaren Schefer, "Non-Violation Complaints in WTO/GATT Dispute Settlement: Past, Present and Future"; Frieder Roessler, "The Concept of Nullification and Impairment in the Legal System of the World Trade Organisation", in Ernst-Ulrich Petersmann (ed.) *International Trade Law and the GATT/WTO Dispute Settlement System* (1997), at 143 and 123, respectively; Ernst-Ulrich Petersmann, "Violation Complaints and Non-Violation Complaints in Public International Trade Law", 34 *German Yearbook of International Law* (1991) 175; Armin von Bogdandy, "The Non-Violation Procedure of Article XXIII:2(b): Its Operational Rationale", 26 *Journal of World Trade* (1992) 95.

[104] Art. XXIII:3 GATS provides: "If any Member considers that any benefit it could reasonably have expected to accrue to it under a specific commitment of another Member under Part III of this Agreement is being nullified or impaired as a result of the application of any measure which does not conflict with the provisions of this Agreement, it may have recourse to the DSU. If the measure is determined by the DSB to have nullified or impaired such a benefit, the Member affected shall be entitled to a mutually satisfactory adjustment on the basis of para. 2 of Art. XXI, which may include the modification or withdrawal of the measure. In the event an agreement cannot be reached between the Members concerned, Art. 22 of the DSU shall apply." It should be noted that, contrary to the GATT provisions on non-violation, GATS Art. XXIII:3 makes explicitly available ordinary remedies under Art. 22 DSU, including cross-retaliation, with regard to non-violation complaints. See Thomas Cottier and Kristina Nadakavukaren Schefer, *supra* n. 103, at 157.

[105] Art. 64 TRIPS. See World Trade Organization, *Non-Violation Complaints and the TRIPS Agreement*, IP/C/W/124, 1999.

[106] Art. 26 DSU.

by another contracting party as a result of the application of any measure, whether or not it conflicts with the General Agreement.[107]

The validity of this assumption today, however, has been questioned, either because the non-violation mechanism has become largely redundant "[i]n the light of the good faith protection in treaty application and interpretation which nowadays prevails in public international law",[108] or because "the broad extension of the multilateral trade order into the area of domestic policies" has reduced the need for such a remedy.[109]

Early GATT Panels have regularly granted non-violation complaints after having found that the superficially origin-neutral measures at hand were not discriminatory, on the basis that the product categories under consideration could not be considered "like," but were nevertheless in a competitive relationship.[110] In this conception, non-violation complaints offer a second-line remedy against origin-neutral domestic regulation which adversely affects the competitive conditions of foreign products/services, but are not considered to constitute *de facto* discrimination. In *Japan—Measures Affecting Consumer Photographic Film and Paper*,[111] the United States had argued along these lines that certain Japanese distribution measures constituted either *de facto* discrimination in breach of GATT Article III:4 or a non-violation nullification and impairment of benefits.[112] The panel made a number of findings that are relevant to defining the borderline between facially origin-neutral measures which should nevertheless be considered *de facto* discriminatory and in breach of the National Treatment obligation, and those which are not.[113] The following considerations should be highlighted in that respect.

First, the panel did not see any significant distinction between *the nullification and impairment standard* applied under Article XXIII:1(b)— that of "upsetting the competitive relationship"—and the standard of "upsetting effective equality of competitive opportunities" applicable to Article III:4, apart from the fact that this Article III:4 standard calls for no

---

[107] Panel report on *EEC—Payments and Subsidies Paid to Processors and Producers of Oilseeds and Related Animal-Feed Proteins* (L/6627, adopted 25 January 1990, BISD 37S/86).

[108] Thomas Cottier and Kristina Nadakavukaren Schefer, *supra* n. 103, at 134–135, and Frieder Roessler, *supra* n. 103, at 180.

[109] Frieder Roessler, *ibid.*

[110] See the panel reports on *The Australian Subsidy On Ammonium Sulphate*, *supra* n. 17; *Treatment By Germany Of Imports Of Sardines* (G/26, adopted 31 October 1952, BISD 1S/53).

[111] Panel Report on *Japan—Measures Affecting Consumer Photographic Film and Paper* (WT/DS44/R, adopted 22 April 1998).

[112] *Ibid.*, para. 4.26.

[113] For an analysis of the *Japan—Film* dispute in general and an analysis of the panel report, see James Durling and Simon Lester, "Original Meanings and the Film Dispute: The Drafting History, Textual Evolution, and Application of the Non-Violation Nullification and Impairment Remedy", 32 *George Washington Journal of International Law* (1999) 211.

less favourable treatment for imported products in general, whereas the Article XXIII:1(b) standard calls for a comparison of the competitive relationship between foreign and domestic products at two specific points in time, i.e., when the concession was granted and currently.[114]

Second, the panel addressed the relevance of the *origin-neutral nature* of a measure to causation of non-violation nullification and impairment. It considered that, even in the absence of *de jure* discrimination, it could be possible for a complainant to show *de facto* discrimination. In such circumstances, however, the complainant must make a detailed showing of any claimed disproportionate impact on imports resulting from the origin-neutral measure.[115] Moreover, the panel considered that, despite the fact that past cases on *de facto* discrimination dealt with GATT provisions other than Article XXIII:1(b), the reasoning contained therein appeared to be equally applicable in addressing the question of *de facto* discrimination with respect to claims of non-violation nullification or impairment.[116] Conversely, the panel rejected the Article III:4 claim by the US "essentially for the reasons already stated in [its] findings on non-violation nullification and impairment."[117]

Third, the panel addressed the relevance of *intent* to causation under non-violation. It noted that Article XXIII:1(b) does not require a proof of intent of nullification or impairment of benefits by a government adopting a measure. What matters for purposes of establishing causality is the impact of a measure, i.e. whether it upsets competitive relationships. Nonetheless, in the panel's view, intent may not be irrelevant. If a measure that appears on its face to be origin-neutral in its effect on domestic and imported products is nevertheless shown to have been intended to restrict imports, the panel suggested it "may be more inclined" to find a causal relationship in specific cases, bearing in mind that intent is not determinative where it in fact exists.[118]

Fourth, as regards the *causation standard* in non-violation complaints, the panel stated that "the issue is whether such a measure has caused nullification or impairment, i.e., whether it has made more than a *de minimis* contribution to nullification or impairment."[119] The panel thus seemed to have accepted the United States' argument that a measure should not be a *sine qua non* ("but for" condition) for a causal link to be shown.[120]

---

[114] Panel report on *Japan—Measures Affecting Consumer Photographic Film and Paper*, *supra* n. 111, para. 10.380.

[115] *Ibid.*, para. 10.85.

[116] *Ibid.*, para. 10.86. The Panel referred to *Japan—Alcoholic Beverages* and *EC—Bananas*.

[117] *Ibid.*, para. 10.381–382.

[118] *Ibid.*, para. 10.87.

[119] *Ibid.*, para. 10.84.

[120] *Ibid.*, para. 6.270.

In *EC—Asbestos* a panel dealt for the first time with a non-violation complaint regarding a domestic regulation pursuing health protection objectives which had been found discriminatory but also justifiable under Article XX. The panel found that the treatment of such measures under GATT Article XXIII:1(b) should be different from purely commercial measures:

> the Panel is of the opinion that even if the justification of a measure by Article XX does not, in principle, make it impossible to invoke Article XXIII:1(b) in relation to the application of the measure justified, the situation of a measure falling under Article XX with respect to Article XXIII:2(b) cannot be quite the same as that of a measure consistent with another provision of the GATT 1994. [. . .] The Panel considers that in accepting the WTO Agreement Members also accept, *a priori*, through the introduction of these general exceptions, that Members will be able, at some point, to have recourse to these exceptions. [. . .] All this leads the Panel to consider that, in practice, [. . .] the risk of an effective increase in the cost of measures necessary to protect public health because of the applicability of Article XXIII:2(b) to measures justified under Article XX can only be very marginal.[121]

The panel went on to argue that this special treatment of measures justified by Article XX should be reflected in the claimant's burden of proof under Article XXIII:2(b), which should be stricter:

> Furthermore, . . . we consider that the special situation of measures justified under Article XX, insofar as they concern non-commercial interests whose importance has been recognized *a priori* by Members, requires special treatment. By creating the right to invoke exceptions in certain circumstances, Members have recognized *a priori* the possibility that the benefits they derive from certain concessions may eventually be nullified or impaired at some future time for reasons recognized as being of overriding importance. This situation is different from that in which a Member takes a measure of a commercial or economic nature such as, for example, a subsidy or a decision organizing a sector of its economy, from which it expects a purely economic benefit. In this latter case, the measure remains within the field of international trade. Moreover, the nature and importance of certain measures falling under Article XX can also justify their being taken at any time, which militates in favour of a stricter treatment of actions brought against them on the basis of Article XXIII:1(b).

> Consequently, the Panel concludes that because of the importance conferred on them *a priori* by the GATT 1994, as compared with the rules governing international trade, situations that fall under Article XX justify a stricter burden of proof being applied in this context to the party invoking Article XXIII:1(b), particularly with regard to the existence of legitimate expectations and whether or not the initial Decree could be reasonably anticipated.[122]

---

[121] Panel report on *European Communities—Measures Affecting Asbestos and Asbestos-Containing Products, supra* n. 27, para. 8.272.

[122] *Ibid.*, paras. 8.281–8.282.

The EC appealed against the panel's findings that (1) Article XXIII:1(b) applies to measures that fall within the scope of application of other provisions of the GATT 1994, and (2) Article XXIII:1(b) applies to measures which pursue health, rather than commercial, objectives and which can, therefore, be justified under Article XX(b) of the GATT 1994. The Appellate Body, however, upheld both findings. As for the first claim, the Appellate Body held that a measure may, at one and the same time, be inconsistent with, or in breach of, a provision of the GATT 1994 *and*, nonetheless, give rise to a cause of action under Article XXIII:1(b). The Appellate Body, however, also added that "[o]f course, if a measure 'conflicts' with a provision of the GATT 1994, that measure must actually fall within the scope of application of that provision of the GATT 1994."[123] As regards the second claim, the Appellate Body opined that the use of the words "*any measure*" in Article XXIII:1(b) suggests that measures of all types may give rise to such a cause of action, and clearly contradicts the European Communities' argument that certain types of measure, namely, those with health objectives, are excluded from the scope of application of Article XXIII:1(b).[124]

---

[123] Appellate Body report on *European Communities—Measures Affecting Asbestos and Asbestos-Containing Products, supra* n. 54, para. 187.
[124] *Ibid.*, para. 188.

4

From Japanese Shoshu to Chilean Pisco: Two Ways to Think about WTO Assessment of Origin-Neutral Regulation

C HAPTERS TWO AND three have introduced the reader to the data. We will now critically assess the outcome and explore an alternative track. In this chapter, we will therefore start by some stock-taking, bringing together the key elements from the previous chapters into a coherent and synthetic presentation, and then move on to summarise our own proposal.

A. STOCK-TAKING: THE *JAPAN—ALCOHOLIC BEVERAGES* TRACK

Some of our findings in the last two chapters can be systematically represented as follows:

Table 1 represents how a WTO panel or the Appellate Body, when confronted with a claim alleging that the domestic regulation at hand nullifies or impairs benefits accruing to a member under the agreement, would have to make one to four analytical determinations, along the lines of the case law described above (assuming the measure can effectively be qualified as a "measure" covered by the relevant provisions):

—*First determination (D_1)*: does the domestic regulation specifically and adversely affect the competitive conditions of foreign goods or services/service suppliers?

—*Second determination (D_2)*: in case adverse effects can be shown to be caused by the domestic regulation, does the measure constitute a violation or can it merely give rise to a non-violation complaint?

—*Third determination (D_3)*: in either case, can the complaining party demonstrate that the domestic regulation has impaired or nullified benefits accruing to it under the agreements?

Table 1. WTO Compliance Assessment of Facially Origin-Neutral Regulation under Traditional GATT/GATS Case Law

	T_1	T_2	D_1	D_2	D_3	D_4
1. GATT	L	ONM	AE	V: Art. III	*prima facie* N&I	Necessity
				?	(Art. 3.8 DSU)	(Art. XX)
				NV	N&I	—
				not reasonably	*de minimis*	
				anticipated	causation	
			no AE			
2. GATT	ONM	L	AE	V: Art. III	*prima facie* N&I	Necessity
				?	(Art. 3.8 DSU)	(Art. XX)
			no AE			
3. GATS	ONM	L	AE	V: Art. XVII	*prima facie* N&I	Necessity
				?	(Art. 3.8 DSU)	(Art. XIV)
			no AE			
4. GATS	L	ONM	AE	V: Art. XVII	*prima facie* N&I	Necessity
				?	(Art. 3.8 DSU)	(Art. XIV)
				V: Art. VI	*prima facie* N&I	Necessity
				not reasonably	(Art. 3.8 DSU)	(Art. XIV)
				anticipated		
				NV	N&I	—
				not reasonably	*de minimis*	
				anticipated	causation	
			no AE			

T= point in time; D= judicial determination; L= multilateral liberalisation; ONM= origin neutral measure; AE= specific adverse effects on competitive conditions of foreign products or services; V= violation; NV= non-violation; N&I= nullification and impairment.

—*Fourth Determination (D₄)*: in the case of a violation, can the domestic regulation be saved under either GATT Article XX or GATS Article XIV?

Table 1 presents the four factual hypotheticals in which some or all of these determinations may have to be made:

—The situation where a domestic regulation has been adopted by a member following multilateral liberalisation commitments under GATT (1).
—The situation where a domestic regulation was in existence prior to the scheduling of commitments under GATT (2).
—The situation where a domestic regulation was in existence prior to the scheduling of commitments under GATS (3).
—The situation where a domestic regulation has been adopted by a member following multilateral liberalisation commitments under the GATS (4).

These distinctions are primarily of importance to the possibility of non-violation complaints. As evidenced by the panel report in *Japan—Film*, a non-violation complaint against a domestic regulation which was in force before the impaired or nullified commitment was scheduled, will entail such a heavy burden of proof for the complainant that it can be assumed, for the purpose of our analysis, that in such a hypothesis a non-violation complaint will fail.[1] The same applies to violation complaints with respect to GATS Article VI:5, which, as we will discuss below, incorporates the substantive elements of a non-violation complaint, in particular the requirement that the domestic regulation at hand "could not reasonably have been expected." This assumption is reflected in table 1 by omitting the possibility for non-violation claims in scenarios (2) and (3).[2]

As for the consecutive judicial determinations, D_1 is the first step in any assessment by a WTO panel or the Appellate Body of the WTO compliance of a domestic regulation. Without evidence of adverse effects there can logically be no violation or non-violation complaint. After *Japan—Film*, it would seem that proving adverse effects requires for both violation and non-violation purposes the upsetting of competitive conditions, and does not require actual effects on trade. D_3 concerns the relationship between a finding of either violation or non-violation and nullification and impairment, and deals with the type of causation required to determine whether a particular domestic regulation has impaired or nullified benefits in the context of either violation or non-violation complaints. It suffices here to recall that a complainant claiming violation of GATT Article III, GATS Article XVII or GATS Article VI:5 will benefit from the rebuttable presumption of nullification and impairment for violation complaints laid down in Article 3.8 DSU, and will not have to demonstrate *de minimis* causation as is the case for non-violation complaints.

---

[1] See panel report on *Japan—Measures Affecting Consumer Photographic Film and Paper* (WT/DS44/R, adopted 22 April 1998), para. 10.80: "in the case of measures shown by Japan to have been introduced prior to the conclusion of the tariff negotiations at issue, it is our view that [the defendant] has raised a presumption that [the claimant] should be held to have anticipated those measures and it is for [the claimant] to rebut that presumption. In this connection, it is our view that [the claimant] is charged with knowledge of [the defendant's] measures as of the date of their publication. We realise that knowledge of a measure's existence is not equivalent to understanding the impact of the measure on a specific product market. [. . .] However, where [the claimant] claims that it did not know of a measure's relevance to market access conditions in respect of [a specific product], we would expect [the claimant] to clearly demonstrate why initially it could not have reasonably anticipated the effect of an existing measure on [a specific product market] and when it did realise the effect."

[2] See Joel Trachtman, "The Domain of WTO Dispute Resolution", 40 *Harvard International Law Journal* (1999) 333, 371, note 176: "This decision sets a high standard for future nullification and impairment cases, refusing to engage in broad criticism of at least long-standing domestic measures that may have the effect of reducing the value of tariff concessions."

The key to our discussion, however, is addressed by D_2. When a domestic regulation has been shown to adversely affect the competitive conditions of foreign products or services/service suppliers, how do we decide whether the regulation constitutes a breach of the National Treatment obligation, or, rather, can at the most support a non-violation claim? Put another way, when a measure adversely affects competitive conditions of foreign products or services/service suppliers, does a WTO panel or Appellate Body need to make any additional findings before concluding to *de facto* discrimination or non-violation? As for the latter, the additional requirement consists of proving that the measure could not have been reasonably anticipated. As for the former, however, things are less clear. At D_2 the arbitrage between trade liberalisation and deep market integration takes place. If each and every measure with adverse effects on foreign products/services would be considered a breach of the National Treatment obligation, the line between non-discrimination and deregulation would *ipso facto* become blurred. But what limitations can be proposed, taking into account the need for legal certainty, on the one hand, and the danger of regulatory protectionism, on the other? As we have seen, consideration of regulatory objectives has been—after *Canada-Periodicals* at least partly—rejected under a GATT Article III:4 or GATS Article XVII analysis. We will argue that the Appellate Body has not been able to provide fully satisfactory guidance in this respect, instead preferring a very casuistic approach continuously swinging from one side of the spectrum to the other and back.

B. OUR PROPOSAL: THE *CHILE—ALCOHOLIC BEVERAGES* TRACK

As we have already stated above, *Chile—Alcoholic Beverages* stands, in our view, for the proposition that National Treatment incorporates a necessity test, at least under GATT Article III:2, second sentence. In the next chapter, we will explain on what grounds a generalisation of this proposition can be supported. An "integrated necessity test", then, could be represented by simply merging D_4 in Table 1 with D_2. This conclusion would follow from the premise, which we will demonstrate below, that, as far as facially origin-neutral measures are concerned,[3] the legitimate policy exception of GATT Article XX and GATS Article XIV is redundant under such a discrimination test since both the chapeau, in relation to a National Treatment violation, and the provisional justification, the

---

[3] We will argue below that origin-specific, i.e. *de jure* discriminatory, measures will continue to be assessed under the legitimate policy exceptions of GATT and GATS.

"connectors," merely lay down, at the most,[4] a necessity test. National Treatment analysis could thus be presented as follows:

Table 2. WTO Compliance Assessment of Origin-Neutral Regulation à la *Chile—Alcoholic Beverages*

	T_1	T_2	D_1	D_2	D_3
1. **GATT**	L	ONM	AE	V: Art. III **Necessity** NV not reasonably anticipated	*prima facie* N&I (Art. 3.8 DSU) N&I *de minimis* causation
2. **GATT**	ONM	L	AE	V: Art. III **Necessity**	*prima facie* N&I (Art. 3.8 DSU)
3. **GATS**	ONM	L	AE	V: Art. XVII **Necessity**	*prima facie* N&I (Art. 3.8 DSU)
4. **GATS**	L	ONM	AE	V: Art. XVII **Necessity** V: Art. VI not reasonably anticipated NV not reasonably anticipated	*prima facie* N&I (Art. 3.8 DSU) *prima facie* N&I (Art. 3.8 DSU) N&I *de minimis* causation

T= point in time; D= judicial determination; L= multilateral liberalisation; ONM= origin neutral measure; AE= specific adverse effects on competitive conditions of foreign products or services; V= violation; NV= non-violation; N&I= nullification and impairment.

This is the outcome of the alternative track. We will now explain why we prefer this track.

---

[4] Other connectors under GATT Art. XX, such as "relating to," lay down a test less strict than necessity. They are thus pre-empted by a necessity test in a causation-based discrimination analysis.

5

Why Equate Non-Discrimination with Necessity?

A. THE INTUITIVE ARGUMENT: SAFEGUARDING REGULATORY AUTONOMY BY REQUIRING REGULATORY EFFICIENCY

THE BASIC RATIONALE underlying our thesis is of an intuitive nature and is pretty straightforward. A State's domestic "regulatory autonomy" encompasses two aspects:

—its autonomy as regards the policy objectives it chooses to pursue; and
—its autonomy as regards the means by which it chooses to pursue such policy objectives.

We take the view that WTO law should not interfere with either aspects of this autonomy, except to the extent that:

—the free choice of a policy objectives amounts to *overt* protectionism; and
—the free choice of regulatory means amounts to *covert* protectionism.

Consequently, WTO law should require Members (1) to advance a policy goal which is not overtly protectionist, and (2) to pursue this policy goal by means which do not reveal covert protectionism. *De jure* discrimination signals an overtly protectionist goal which can be readily discerned from the text, whereas *de facto* discrimination will, by definition, pursue a purported non-protectionist goal and can only be "discovered" by examining the relation between the means and the end.

Trying to tackle *de facto* discrimination in a two-step mechanism (like GATT Articles III–XX or GATS Articles XVII–XIV) is therefore not only *impossible* (because it requires means–end examination), it is also *dangerous* for Members' regulatory autonomy: it unavoidably leads to a restriction of a Member's choice of policy objectives to the exhaustive[1] list of GATT Article XX/GATS Article XIV. The WTO, however, is not

---

[1] Unless the purported legitimate objective can be brought under the cover of para. (d) of Art. XX.

concerned with the choice of policy objectives,[2] but with the choice of regulatory instruments. The panel in *Chile—Alcoholic Beverages* explicitly confirmed this, when it stated that "while [the Panel] will not examine the stated objective itself to determine its legitimacy, it is a relevant inquiry to examine the *relationship* between the stated objective and the measure in question."[3] The panel's analysis was restricted to GATT Article III:2, second sentence, and is, according to the Appellate Body, not transferable to either GATT Article III:4 or GATS Article XVII. In this section, we will advance a number of policy and legal arguments in support of the thesis that (1) for *any and all* of these National Treatment provisions (2) the adequate means-end analysis is an integrated *necessity* test.

B.   REMEDYING THE FLAWS AND FAILURES OF EXISTING CASE LAW: ADDING
SOME RULE TO THE STANDARD

In our view, a number of egregious inconsistencies can be observed in the current case law defining the interface between WTO law and domestic regulation. Basically, it lacks transparency and consistency, thereby affecting its legitimacy. The acceptance of an integrated necessity test would remedy these inconsistencies, and enhance its legitimacy by making the judicial decision-making process more transparent and verifiable. In this chapter, we will first outline our major problems with the current case law, and then move on to describe the benefits of replacing it with our proposal.

1. **Insufficiently Transparent and Consistent: GATT/WTO Case Law Defining the Interface between the WTO and Domestic Legal Orders**

(a) Likeness

The panel and Appellate Body case law on the relevance of regulatory objectives and likeness has been subject to stinging criticism, and rightly so. Whereas the panel in *United States—Taxes on Automobiles* had set

---

[2] Of course, a means–end assessment, such as a necessity test, requires that the regulating Member articulates what end, i.e. what precise policy goal, it is pursuing. In the case of environment, health and safety protection, for instance, it may be necessary to require a Member to indicate its "appropriate level of protection" (ALOP). The Appellate Body has indeed ruled that Members are implicitly obliged under the SPS Agreement to determine their ALOP with sufficient precision. See Appellate Body report on *Australia—Measure concerning the Importation of Salmon* (WT/DS18/AB/R, adopted 6 November 1998), para. 207.

[3] Panel report on *Chile—Taxes on Alcoholic Beverages* (WT/DS87/R, adopted 12 January 2000), para 7.148, original emphasis.

the door wide open for regulatory protectionism under GATT, the panels and Appellate Body decisions in and after *Japan—Alcoholic Beverages*, while embodying a genuine attempt to shut the protectionist door again, are intellectually flawed on several accounts. Although they surely remedied the most poignant legal shortcomings of the aims-and-effects case law under GATT, the judicial U-turns taken in and after *Japan—Alcoholic Beverages* therefore are not entirely satisfactory either.[4]

The aims-and-effects test which was professed in *United States— Taxes on Automobiles* is to be considered overly permissive of regulatory barriers. It has been suggested that the panel was influenced by the then ongoing congressional debate on US membership in the WTO.[5] Although the panel Report has merit in drawing attention to the fact that "[regulatory] burdens are often distributed according to fortuitous market circumstances,"[6] hence—in our view—rightly urging caution when defining the scope of *de facto* discrimination, it set the standard for finding a breach of Article III excessively high by introducing the "inherence" criterion. According to this criterion, a domestic regulation would only be found to have an adverse effect on competitive opportunities if a certain production *capability* is inherently confined to domestic producers, i.e. if foreign producers could not change their production plan, possibly away from where their comparative advantage lies, in order to accede to a less burdensome regulatory category which benefits domestic producers. One can easily find double fault with this reasoning.[7] First, by requiring that foreign producers change their specialisation for them to receive the same treatment as domestic producers, their competitive opportunities are *ipso facto* adversely affected, since such a change will generally entail considerable costs. Second, if the specialisation of the foreign producer reflects its comparative advantage, the inherence criterion denies the very basis of international trade by requiring the foreign producer to move away from it. In short, the panel basically gave *carte blanche* to anyone who felt like closing her market to imports.

---

[4] The harshest critique on the panel report on *Japan—Taxes on Alcoholic Beverages* was delivered by Robert Hudec, "GATT/WTO Constraints on Domestic Regulation: Requiem for an 'Aims and Effects' Test", 32 *The International Lawyer* (1998) 623.

[5] James Snelson, "Can Article III recover from its Head-On Collision with United States—Taxes on Automobiles?", 5 *Minnesota Journal of Global Trade* (1996) 467, 468.

[6] Robert Hudec, *supra* n. 4 at 639.

[7] See James Snelson, *supra* n. 4, at 492–493: "The Panel's view of inherence disregards economic reality. [. . .] A foreign producer who, in response to new taxes or domestic regulations, "chooses" to change or expand its market specialisation provides a significant competitive advantage to "lucky" domestic producers whose market specialisations are unaffected by the new measures." See also Aaditya Mattoo, "Regulatory Autonomy and Multilateral Disciplines: The Dilemma and a Possible Resolution", 1 *Journal of International Economic Law* (1998) 303, 311: "if any foreign production exists or *could exist* in the product category subject to higher taxes, it would be impossible to find protectionist intent or effect."

The Appellate Body in *Japan—Alcoholic Beverages* therefore rightly approved of the panel's rejection of the aims-and-effects test, but it did not, in our view, succeed in explaining the role of Article III:1 in a very consistent manner. It correctly stated that the first paragraph is part of the context of all other paragraphs of Article III. It failed, however, to give a meaningful interpretation to the explicit reference in the second sentence of Article III:2 to Article III:1. According to the Appellate Body, this explicit reference meant that a *distinct* "protective application" test needed to be applied when considering the consistency of tax measures with the second sentence. Apart from the intellectual awkwardness of this "protective application" test *per se*—we will come back to this below—it must be observed that the Appellate Body's interpretation of the explicit reference to Article III:1 is highly artificial. The result is now that in relation to the second sentence, one has to show "something" *more*—"protective application," not intent—to establish a violation, but one does not need to establish this in relation to the first sentence. A tax measure will be in breach of the first sentence when (1) the products are like, and (2) there is taxation "in excess of."

One can sympathise with a young judicial institution like the Appellate Body for treading cautiously in relation to the interpretation of key provisions such as Article III.[8] However, in *Japan—Alcoholic Beverages* it could have interpreted the Article III:1 reference in Article III:2, second sentence differently, without therefore going beyond a textual interpretation and embarking on such an artificial line of reasoning. An alternative interpretation which, in our view, makes more sense would have consisted of the following. The first sentence of Article III:2 clearly sets a precise standard of violation: to tax "in excess of." The second sentence, however, creates a *residual* category of violations, i.e. violations not involving taxation "in excess of," by prohibiting the taxation of imported products "otherwise" "in a manner contrary to the principles set forth in paragraph 1." The Ad Note to Article III:2 clarifies that "otherwise" "in a manner contrary to the principles set forth in Article III:1" should be understood as meaning "not similarly." This makes perfect sense, since one does not see how taxing imported products "otherwise" could have a protective effect if they are taxed in the same way. The Appellate Body has rightly interpreted the second sentence in light of the Ad Note as requiring more than a *de minimis* difference of tax treatment. But why did it construct the reference to Article III:1 as an additional standard? In our view, *both* taxation "in excess of" with regard to like products and taxation "not similarly" with regard to DCS products can be construed in a meaningful way as specific applications of the same general injunction in Article III:1 not to afford protection. The explicit reference to Article

---

[8] Robert Hudec, *supra* n. 4, at 633.

III:1 in the second sentence simply gives meaning to the residual category of taxing "otherwise," which would be void of any specificity without this reference.

Arguably, by inventing the "protective application" test, the Appellate Body has tried to strike a balance between adopting a rigorously textual approach and allowing itself some flexibility in future assessments under Article III:2, second sentence. Sure enough, it desperately tried to emphasise that the test is not a matter of protective intent, but a question of protective application, the latter requiring a "comprehensive and objective analysis" of the measure's "design, architecture, and revealing structure." But it does not take a lawyer to see that the Appellate Body was in reality using one and the same standard to distinguish the legal and illegal measures: that is, regulatory intent. Robert Hudec has observed in this respect that the Appellate Body has simply refused to formally support an aims-and-effects test, while covertly using this very test in its own analysis:

> Tribunals usually call for [subjective] discretion when they are being asked to resolve important issues under legal criteria that make little or no policy sense. The normal response of most tribunals to such a task is to decide the case as best as they can by making a seat-of-the-pants judgement about whether the defendant government is behaving correctly or incorrectly—a process of judgement known in some circles as the "smell test." Once the tribunal comes to a conclusion about who should win, it fashions an analysis, in terms of the meaningless criteria it has been asked to apply, that makes the case come out that way.[9]

The question, thus, is not: does regulatory intent matter? When one assumes that *any* domestic regulation may have more adverse *effects* on the competitive opportunities of foreign producers because this is simply inherent to the foreign character of the latter, defining discrimination exclusively in terms of regulatory effects—as proposed by the Appellate Body[10]—will cause the line between non-discrimination and deregulation to be easily blurred, unless an additional criterion—a subjective one like regulatory intent or another, more objective one—can somehow come into play. The dilemma is how to reveal regulatory intent in an acceptable manner or, alternatively, how to define a more adequate criterion which can limit the scope of de facto discrimination in an acceptable manner. The Appellate Body implicitly but surely acknowledged this reality when it talked about the "revealing" structure of a measure as a means to determine whether it was being applied so as to afford protection. The reader of this phrase can only wonder: revealing what? The

---

[9] *Ibid.*, at 634.
[10] The Appellate Body stated in its report (WT/DS8/AB/R, adopted 1 November 1996), p. 27, that "[i]t is irrelevant that protectionism was not an intended objective [. . .]."

answer is, protective intent, of course. The concept of "protective application" is nothing but a painfully far-fetched attempt to define objective parameters which may be revealing of subjective intent.

A primary goal of the multilateral trading system is to create certainty and predictability in order to lower transaction costs. The discretionary margin for the judicial interpretation of key concepts such as National Treatment should therefore be as narrow as reasonably possible, and the resulting case law consistent. It is in this respect crucial that an objective criterion can be defined which narrows the discretionary margin *ex ante*. The panel in *Japan—Alcoholic Beverages* quite rightly decided that this criterion can not consist of statements in legislative preparatory work. One can only regret that the Appellate Body in *Canada—Certain Measures concerning Periodicals* had recourse to exactly such statements to support its findings, hence adding more confusion to the debate.

With respect to Article III:4, the Appellate Body recently appears to have chosen yet another track. First, after having rejected in *EC— Bananas* the use of its "protective application" test under Article III:4, hence making it a nude effects-based discrimination test, the Appellate Body ruled in *EC—Asbestos* that the association by consumers with a product of a health risk may be indicative of unlikeness. Since the Appellate Body considered that the behaviour of consumers would be influenced by their perception of a health risk, and such consumer behaviour is one of the four traditional criteria determinant of likeness, consumer perception of health risks with respect to a product may result in denying likeness to it. In all fairness to the Appellate Body, it emphasised that all four criteria needed to be weighed, and that the *mere* perception by consumers of a health risk is therefore not necessarily sufficient to make two products unlike. However, it did not indicate either whether products which have the same physical characteristics could still be made "unlike" on the basis of consumer preferences, including consumer perception of a health risk.[11] It only said that if their physical characteristics are *not* the same, a very heavy burden of proof would rest on the Member trying to establish on the basis of consumer preferences that the products *are* nevertheless like.

Interestingly, then, the Appellate Body started off its likeness analysis by noting that the "dictionary definition of 'like' does not indicate *from*

---

[11] Along the same lines, Howse and Tuerk posit that "the AB does *not* say that, where the analysis of physical characteristics points towards *likeness*, the burden of establishing *un*likeness on the basis of *other* criteria and evidence is especially heavy. Thus, whatever the merits of the AB's prioritisation of physical characteristics, the AB is not deploying that prioritisation in such a way as to reinforce the notion that products cannot normally be unlike once it has been established that they are physically 'like'." Robert Howse and Elisabeth Tuerk, "The WTO Impact on Internal Regulations—A Case Study of the Canada–EC Asbestos Dispute", in Grainne De Burca And Joanne Scott (eds.) *The EU and the WTO: Legal and Constitutional Aspects* (Hart Publishing, Oxford, 2001), at 304.

whose perspective 'likeness' should be judged."[12] The Appellate Body did not care to explicitly answer this paramount question in its analysis, but its considerations regarding consumers' perception of health risks appear to suggest that, at the end of the day, it is the consumer's perspective which should be determinant. As Howse and Tuerk put it,

> This sort of analysis of consumer tastes and behaviour brings into the picture the kinds of regulatory interests, which had under the GATT been taken into account through the "aims and effects" test. It is just that those interests are taken into account here not by adopting the perspective of the regulator as such, but the perspective of consumer behaviour in an idealised market-place.[13]

Although it seems, a priori, very laudable that such weight is given to consumer preferences, arguably the closest proxy for cross-price elasticity, the ruling also raises a major dilemma. It potentially allows a health risk evaluation by the consumer, which is void of any scientific underpinning, to justify a domestic regulation which specifically and adversely affects imports. This is problematic because consumer behaviour is naturally exposed to influence by government. There are boundaries to consumer autonomy. A simple example can clarify this. Assume that in a particular country ten years ago imports of hormone-treated beef were banned on the basis that consumption of such beef would pose a health risk. Assume also that this ban was not supported by any scientific evidence. Is it not reasonable to assume that, after ten years of government warnings against the allegedly hazardous beef, many citizens of that country will be convinced that the beef *is* indeed hazardous? Another example. Assume that a particular government has decided to ban imports of genetically modified foodstuffs, following the launching of a discreet but effective GMO food scare campaign by the agricultural lobbies in that country. Assume that there is no scientific evidence supporting the ban. Who will consumers in that country continue to believe: foreign exporters or their own government? The answer, in our view, is quite likely to be the latter. Thus, governments may very well be tempted to "inform" their citizens of a "health risk" in relation to certain imports, and succeed in turning consumers against those imports. As a result, governments, who *are* accountable under WTO law, would be allowed to discreetly shift the job of protecting domestic industry to the consumers, who, of course, are *not* accountable under WTO law. The line between "Buy Domestic" campaigns and frivolous, scientifically uninformed health regulation is indeed very thin.

Along these lines, in *EC—Asbestos* Canada had made the argument that consumer preferences in France had been altered or even

---

[12] Appellate Body report on *European Communities—Measures Affecting Asbestos and Asbestos-Containing Products* (WT/DS135/AB/R, adopted 5 April 2001), para. 92. Original emphasis.

[13] Robert Howse and Elisabeth Tuerk, *supra* n. 11, at 301.

suppressed by regulatory action. The Appellate Body, however, dismissed this argument on two grounds. First, Canada could submit evidence of "latent, or suppressed consumer demand" in the market, referring to its report in *Korea—Alcohol*.[14] In that report,[15] the Appellate Body stated that studies of cross-price elasticity can be used to predict the change in demand that would result from *a change in the price* of a product following, *inter alia*, from a change in the relative tax burdens on domestic and imported products. Thus, such studies could be used to demonstrate that demand for the imported product would increase, should it become more *price-competitive*. In our view, however, in the case of demand which has been suppressed under the guise of health protection, even if the imported product were to become more *price-competitive*, this would still not alter the fact that, because of governmental brain-washing, demand for the allegedly hazardous product may still not increase for *non-price-competitive* reasons, i.e. the perceived health risk. The burden of proof on Canada was, therefore, impossible to meet, and the Appellate Body's argument is not persuasive.

Second, according to the Appellate Body, Canada could have submitted "evidence of substitutability from some relevant third market".[15a] Put another way, the particular risk perception by consumers in one country should be a relevant criterion to determine whether a particular imported product is to be considered like a domestic product in another country. We fail to see how this argument can be reconciled with the proposition that each WTO Member determines its own level of protection: allowing for consideration of the subjective risk perception by the consumer constituency of one Member to determine whether regulation in another Member is permissible protection of that Member's consumer constituency appears to negate Members' right to choose their own level of protection.

By making these observations, we do not mean to detract from the importance of consumer preferences in the assessment of likeness. We consider, however, that, in the absence of an integrated necessity test in National Treatment analysis, WTO Members may feel invited by the Appellate Body ruling in the *EC—Asbestos* to delegate protectionism to their consumer constituencies.

Equally problematic is the case law on likeness of services and service suppliers under GATS. *EC—Bananas* offered the panel and Appellate Body a first opportunity to address the pristine likeness issue under

---

[14] Appellate Body report on *European Communities—Measures Affecting Asbestos and Asbestos-Containing Products*, *supra* n. 12, para. 123.

[15] Appellate Body report on *Korea—Taxes on Alcoholic Beverages* (WT/DS75/AB/R, adopted 17 February 1999), para. 121.

[15a] Appellate Body report on *European Communities—Measures Affecting Asbestos and Asbestos-Containing Products*, *supra* n. 12, para. 123.

GATS. As noted above, they did so in a remarkably summary or even cryptic fashion. One commentator has observed in this respect, "[t]he scarcity of this reasoning is inversely related to the precedential value of this finding for future cases involving trade in services."[16] Although it has been suggested that this may be due to the fact that the parties to the dispute themselves had only addressed the issue *en passant*,[17] it is probably more plausible to assume that the drafters of the panel report were very wary of opening this tremendously rich Pandora's box. In that box are hidden several dimensions of likeness: likeness of services; likeness of service suppliers; and the interface between those two.

Likeness is certainly the most prominent feature of the National treatment obligation where the goods–services transplant may require quite some judicial creativity for the rights and obligations of WTO members to be clearly delineated, and the transplant to work. WTO Panels and the Appellate Body after *EC—Bananas* will undoubtedly have to revisit the issue. In doing so, they will find the likeness of services *per se* to be the least controversial concept to define. Surely, they will need to define criteria for determining likeness somewhat different from those applied to goods. As observed by Mattoo, most of the traditional likeness criteria for goods, i.e. customs classification and physical characteristics, are of no or limited use in the services context, with the exception of end-uses, which incorporates the notion of substitutability.[18] Application of the latter criterion, however, should result in meaningful distinctions as regards intra-mode comparisons.[19] But even here it will not always be easy to draw the line. What to say, for example, about the underwriting of a bond issue and a bank lending transaction?[20] Or "ethical" investment funds as opposed to investment funds which have not pledged the same commitment? Can these service products said to be like for regulatory purposes?

These examples assumed that the relevant services are being delivered through the same mode, i.e. either cross-border or through commercial presence. Making inter-mode comparisons between services entails the

---

[16] Werner Zdouc, "WTO Dispute Settlement Practice Relating to the GATS", 4 *Journal of International Economic Law* (1999) 295, 332.

[17] *Ibid.*, 333.

[18] The services classification list, as embodied in WTO document MTN.GNS/W/120 (currently under review), is far too rudimentary to provide the same guidance as the harmonised system classification for goods. Physical characteristics are of no help when it comes to determining the likeness of intangible services. See, extensively, Aaditya Mattoo, "MFN and the GATS", in Thomas Cottier, Petros Mavroidis, Patrick Blatter (eds.) *Regulatory Barriers and the Principle of Non-Discrimination of World Trade Law: Past, Present and Future* (1999). The author reiterated a position publicly defended earlier in a seminal piece, *supra* n. 7, at 127.

[19] *Ibid.*

[20] Kalypso Nicolaides and Joel Trachtman, "From Policed Regulation to Managed Recognition: Mapping the Boundary in GATS", paper presented at the *Services 2000: New Directions in Trade Liberalisation* conference, Washington DC, 1999 (on file with the author), at 12.

additional complication of determining the relevance of the mode of delivery in the likeness determination. As discussed in detail by Mattoo, the GATS scheduling methodology allows members to make different National Treatment commitments under the four delivery modes. They can commit to full National Treatment under mode 3 for a particular sector, but refuse National Treatment under mode 1. Thus, the National treatment under GATS can effectively be fragmented over the various modes by the scheduling methodology.[21] However, when a member has scheduled a full National Treatment under all four modes, can it still apply more burdensome regulation to the same service when it is delivered through one mode rather another? Put another way, is a service provided cross-border like the same service provided through commercial presence?[22] As we will see later, in the context of disputes regarding Article 49 of the Treaty of Rome, the ECJ has constantly held that Member States can not necessarily require a cross-border service supplier (i.e. GATS mode 1) to comply with all the regulatory requirements imposed on service suppliers who wish to establish themselves (i.e. GATS mode 3). In *Webb*, for instance, the ECJ held that the principle of non-discrimination

> does not mean that all national legislation applicable to nationals of that State and usually applied to the permanent activities of undertakings established therein may be similarly applied in its entirety to the temporary activities of undertakings which are established in other member states.[23]

Could a similar construction be applied against the background of WTO law? The answer to this question depends undoubtedly on how we colour the concept of non-discrimination in WTO law.

The likeness exercise under GATS becomes even more difficult when it comes to determining the likeness of service suppliers and the relevance of the correlation between likeness of service suppliers and likeness of services. The panel in *EC—Bananas* has posited that service suppliers are like to the extent they are like service suppliers.[24] This would, in our view, inevitably, imply that domestic regulators can distinguish between services on the basis of the service characteristics, but *not* on the basis of service supplier characteristics. This is a remarkable finding, since most

---

[21] Aaditya Mattoo, *supra* n. 18, 119–21.

[22] Related to this problem is the issue of technological neutrality: is a service provided by electronic mail different from the same service delivered by regular mail? Is wire-based voice telephony unlike radio-based voice telephony? A consensus appears to be emerging in this respect among WTO members that the means of service delivery should not affect the likeness of otherwise same services. See Patrick Low and Aaditya Mattoo, "Is There a Better Way? Alternative Approaches to Liberalisation under the GATS", mimeo (on file with the author), 1999, 7.

[23] Case 279/80, [1981] ECR 3305, para. 16.

[24] Panel report on *EC—Regime for the Importation, Sale and Distribution of Bananas* (WT/DS27/R, adopted 25 September 1997), para. 7.322.

services regulation is not directed at the characteristics of the service product as such, but, rather, the characteristics of the service supplier supplying that particular service.[25] Saying that the likeness of service suppliers is wholly dependent on, and determined by, the likeness of their services, would go far beyond non-discrimination and impose absurd levels of deregulation on members. The latter would be effectively impeded from making regulatory distinctions between service suppliers offering like services. A domestic solvent bank offering a commercial loan and a foreign bank on the verge of bankruptcy offering the same loan would be like service suppliers and can, in principle, not be treated differently by the financial regulator. A domestic dominant voice telephony service supplier and a foreign new entrant supplying like services would be like suppliers and should, in principle, not be treated differently by the domestic antitrust authorities. One can think of many other examples of that kind.

This definition by the *EC—Bananas* panel has already provoked a number of comments in literature. Zdouc, noting that the panel refused to take supplier-related factors into consideration, observed in this respect, "[a]t second glance, [. . .] the panel's approach to keeping its finding as *narrow* as possible has potentially exactly the *opposite effect* because upon closer consideration the panel's finding concerning the '*likeness*' of service suppliers could also entail an exceedingly *broad* notion of which service suppliers could be considered '*like.*' "[26] Davey and Pauwelyn similarly conclude that "it is arguable that a rather broad view was thus taken."[27] Mattoo, who in 1997 had already argued in

[25] This follows from the fact that most services are intangible and that their externalities can only be addressed by regulating the "producer" of the service. See Alexandre Bernel, *Le Principe d'Equivalence ou de "Reconnaissance Mutuelle" en Droit Communautaire* (1996) 95: "Les services ne prennent naissance que lors de leur exécution. [. . .] Ainsi, par opposition à la pratique en matière de marchandises, un contrôle préalable des caractéristiques des services eux-mêmes n'est guère concevable. *C'est sur la personne du prestataire, voire sur les modalités de son activité que porteront les vérifications antérieures à l'exécution de la prestation.* Les autorités nationales procèdent, d'une part, à un examen des aptitudes des personnes physiques prestataires, concrétisé par l'obtention d'un diplôme de formation ou d'un certificat attestantl'acquisition d'une expérience professionnelle particulière; elles contrôlent, d'autre part, la structure orgasitionnelle ou la capacité financière des entreprises de services, le plus souvent en vue de l'octroi d'une licence d'activité." (emphasis added) See also Aly K Abu-Akeel, "The MFN as it Applies to Services Trade: New Problems for an Old Concept", 33 *Journal of World Trade* (1999) 103, 110; and in the EC context, Giuliano Marenco, "The Notion of Restriction on the Freedom of Establishment and Provision of Services in the Case Law of the Court", *Yearbook of European Law* (1992) 111: "[. . .] the regulation of services by the States [. . .] is more often directed to the *person* providing the service than to the service itself. In general it is not easy to regulate a service as such." (original emphasis)

[26] Werner Zdouc, "WTO Dispute Settlement Practice Relating to the GATS", 4 *Journal of International Economic Law* (1999) 295, 332. Original emphasis. The author also notes that this definition will enhance the liberalising effect of the GATS. *Ibid.*, 333.

[27] Bill Davey and Joost Pauwelyn, "MFN Unconditionality: A Legal Analysis of the Concept in View of its Evolution in the GATT/WTO Jurisprudence with Particular

favour of the definition now adopted by the panel,[28] maintains that one should start from the presumption that all service suppliers offering like services are like, but adds that any distinction between suppliers hence presumed to be like would need to be justified on the basis of an efficiency test.[29] Nicolaides and Trachtman, on the other hand, have suggested to separate the evaluation of treatment of services from the evaluation of treatment of service suppliers. In their view, there should be no violation of National Treatment if like services were treated differently where the reason for the difference in treatment is the regulation of the service supplier, as service supplier. Such an approach would replicate a kind of product/process distinction as a service/service supplier distinction.[30] Writing in Fall 1999, they conclude, "[t]his is likely to be the interpretation that a WTO panel or the Appellate Body would apply".[31]

In our view, the panel in *EC—Bananas* has ruled out even the possibility of differentiation between service suppliers, on the basis of their characteristics "as service suppliers." In the panel's interpretation, if a domestic regulator were to accord different treatment to different supplier categories supplying like services, in a manner which *de facto* adversely affects the competitive conditions of foreign suppliers, there would be a breach of the National Treatment obligation. For instance, if a foreign lawyer established in country Y wishes to provide legal representation services to a client in country X, and is denied the possibility to do so because of his lack of adequate training in Country X's legal system necessary to ensure quality of service, the panel's reasoning would suggest this constitutes a breach of GATS Article XVII. It goes without

Reference to the Issue of 'Like Product' ," in Thomas Cottier and Petros Mavroidis (eds.) *Regulatory Barriers and the Principle of Non-Discrimination in World Trade Law* (2000), at 36. The authors continue, "[i]rrespective of whether a supplier is a natural person or a multinational company, a branch or a subsidiary, a reputable company or a company on the verge of collapse, as long as both supply like services, they will be considered to be like service suppliers."

[28] Aaditya Mattoo, *supra* n. 7, at 133.

[29] Aaditya Mattoo, "MFN and the GATS", in Thomas Cottier, Petros Mavroidis, Patrick Blatter (eds.) *Regulatory Barriers and the Principle of Non-Discrimination of World Trade Law: Past, Present and Future* at 26.

[30] Apart from questioning the validity of the largely doctrinal product/process distinction under GATT, we wonder how this would apply to services. As indicated above, with respect to services trade, the regulation of the "product," i.e. the service, can often not be dissociated from the "process," i.e. the service supplier. The process method is almost always incorporated in the resulting product. The characteristics of the service are often affected by the characteristics of the service supplier. An unqualified professional is most likely to deliver a service which is different from a service delivered by a qualified one. For a powerful challenge to the product/process distinction under GATT, see Robert Howse and Don Regan, "The Product/Process distinction—An Illusory Basis for Disciplining Unilateralism in Trade Policy", 11 *European Journal of International Law* (2000) 249.

[31] Kalypso Nicolaides and Joel Trachtman, *supra* n. 20, at 14. The authors' manuscript is dated September 24, 1999, i.e. exactly two years after the adoption of the *EC—Bananas* Appellate Body report.

saying that the panel's position is untenable. The drafters of the GATS can not have meant to strip domestic regulators from their power to regulate service suppliers in a non-discriminatory manner.

But how should likeness in the services context then be interpreted? One author has suggested the matter can only be resolved by the Council for Trade in Services issuing clear guidelines on the matter.[32] We do not agree. We are convinced that improper weight is being given to the likeness issue. It is widely felt that an origin-neutral regulation should not be stricken down under a National Treatment obligation merely because it renders market access more difficult. As a result, many have viewed likeness as the only means to restrict the—by definition—open-ended nature of an effects-based *de facto* discrimination test. They fear that an effects-based discrimination test is bound to degenerate in deregulation, and want to manipulate the basis of comparison (likeness) in order to impose *ex ante* limits on the standard (adverse effects). Although we fully endorse the objective, we reject the use of likeness as a proper means to that end. The problem needs to be tackled at the source, i.e. a proper understanding of the standard.

We will argue below that an integrated necessity test would largely circumvent the controversy surrounding likeness. The role of likeness can be deflated to its natural proportions within this theory: likeness of services, as a basis of comparison, should be determined using cross-price elasticity, whereas the likeness of service suppliers can be perfectly well defined as a function of the likeness of services. Of course, by the latter we endorse the *EC—Bananas* panel's finding that the likeness of service suppliers follows from the likeness of services, but we do so only partly, namely *provided that* the discrimination standard is properly circumscribed, i.e. using an integrated necessity test, something which the panel obviously failed to do. Using likeness as a shelter for introducing regulatory intent in non-discrimination analysis is troublesome. As stated earlier, likeness does not allow regulatory intent to be revealed in an objective manner. When in other investment-related instruments[33] likeness "was an issue," it was often the result of either exceptional pressures,[34] or particularities invalidating a comparison

---

[32] Aly K. Abu-Akeel, *supra* n. 25, at 115.

[33] We refer to investment-related instruments because of the analogue with GATS mode 3.

[34] In the last draft text of the infamous Multilateral Agreement on Investment (MAI), the Chairman had attempted to meet Civil Society's concerns regarding the open-ended scope of *de facto* discrimination vis-a-vis origin-neutral environmental regulation, by proposing an interpretative note to the National Treatment provision. The proposed interpretative note acknowledges that policy objectives may affect the likeness of circumstances, and emphasises that "*[t]he fact that a measure applied by a government has a different effect on an investment or an investment of another Party would not in itself render the measure inconsistent with National Treatment [. . .].*" OECD, *The MAI Negotiating Text*, 24 April 1998, at 143. Retrievable from http://www.oecd.org. For a sample of the MAI literature, see the

with GATS.[35] In addition, as we will see further on, likeness has never been an analytical stumbling block in the ECJ's rulings on non-discrimination either under the Treaty's provisions on the freedom to provide services or freedom of establishment.

(b) The Relationship National Treatment—Legitimate Policy Exceptions

Surprisingly little attention has been devoted in the past to the structural interface between the National Treatment obligation in GATT and GATS, on the one hand, and the conditions to be fulfilled by a measure to qualify for either a legitimate policy objective or—as we will argue below—a non-violation complaint, on the other. As for the former, the National

symposium issue, "The International Regulation of Foreign Direct Investment: Obstacles and Evolution", 31 *Cornell International Law Journal* (1998) 455, with various contributions on the MAI's National Treatment obligation. See also Gaëtan Verhoosel, "Foreign Direct Investment and Legal Constraints on Domestic Environmental Policies: Striking a 'Reasonable' Balance Between Stability and Change", 29 *Georgetown Journal of Law and Policy in International Business* (1998) 451.

[35] The National Treatment Instrument (NTI) of the OECD, which is part of the Declaration on International Investment and Multinational Enterprises of 1976, for instance, urges Member countries to accord to foreign-controlled enterprises operating in their territories treatment no less favourable than that accorded "in like circumstances" to domestic enterprises. This phrase, inspired on US BITs practice was originally also suggested with regard to national treatment of service suppliers in the Chairman's July 1990 draft of the GATS, but preference was eventually given to "like" service suppliers (see Terence Stewart, *The Uruguay Round: A Negotiating History* (1993)). In OECD practice, foreign investors and domestic enterprises will only be considered to be in like circumstances if they are operating in the same sector. This is similar to the *EC—Bananas* Panel requirement that service suppliers must provide like services to be like. However, contrary to the *EC—Bananas* ruling, "[m]ore general considerations, such as the policy objectives of member countries, could be taken into account to define the circumstances in which comparisons between foreign-controlled and domestic enterprises is permissible inasmuch as those objectives are not contrary to the principle of national Treatment. In any case, the key to determining whether a discriminatory measure applied to foreign-controlled enterprises constitutes an exception to National Treatment is to ascertain whether the discrimination is motivated, at least in part, by the fact that the enterprises concerned are under foreign control." This allowance for consideration of regulatory intent under likeness, however, is due to the fact that the NTI does not provide for a general legitimate exception provision à la GATS Art. XIV (see OECD, *National Treatment for Foreign-Controlled Enterprises* (1991) 22 and United Nations Centre on Transnational Corporations, *Key Concepts in International Investment Arrangements and their Relevance to Negotiations on International Transactions in Services* (1990) 16).
    On the other hand, in the context of the Energy Charter Treaty (ECT) negotiations, the United States and Canada had issued a formal declaration along these lines regarding Art. 10 of the ECT. This provision contains the ECT's National Treatment obligation but does not refer to likeness or like circumstances at all. In their declaration, these States had therefore stated that a comparison between a foreign and domestic undertaking for the purpose of determining the discriminatory character of a domestic regulation will only be valid if the undertakings are in "similar" circumstances. They submitted that such a determination would need to take account of two factors: first, legitimate policy objectives which may justify differential treatment of foreign investors; and second, the motivation behind the measure. Neither the US nor Canada eventually signed up to the ECT (see *Energy Charter Treaty Secretariat, The Energy Charter Treaty and Related Documents* (1995) 33–34).

Treatment obligation in GATT and GATS prohibits discrimination, whereas GATT Article XX/GATS Article XIV allow such discrimination for legitimate purposes, provided the measure does not amount to an unjustifiable or arbitrary discrimination. One would expect these standards, at least partially, to overlap. This would inevitably lead to an erosion of the legitimate policy exception. How then needs the relationship between the two standards defined? The Appellate Body has opined in this respect that:

> [t]he enterprise of applying Article XX would clearly be an unprofitable one if it involved no more than applying the standard used in finding that the [measure at hand was] inconsistent with Article III:4. [. . .] The provisions of the Chapeau cannot logically refer to the same standard(s) by which a violation of a substantive rule has been determined to have occurred. To proceed down that path would be both to empty the Chapeau of its contents and to deprive the exceptions in paragraphs (a) to (j) of meaning. Such recourse would also confuse the question of whether inconsistency with a substantive rule existed, with the further and separate question arising under the chapeau of Article XX as to whether that inconsistency was nevertheless justified. One of the corollaries of the "general rule of interpretation" in the *Vienna Convention* is that interpretation must give meaning and effect to all the terms of a treaty. An interpreter is not free to adopt a reading that would result in reducing whole clauses or paragraphs of a treaty to redundancy or inutility.[36]

All fine and jolly, but *what* exactly is then the difference between those two standards? The reasonably circumspect reader would offer at this point, "the arbitrary or unjustifiable character, of course!" But that would be too easy. In its most recent dictum on the matter, the Appellate Body held,

> The nature and quality of this discrimination is different from the discrimination in the treatment of products which was already found to be inconsistent with one of the substantive obligations of the GATT, such as Article [. . .] III. *Second*, the discrimination must be *arbitrary* or *unjustifiable* in character. (first emphasis added, second and third original)[37]

Hence, the difference between the discrimination standards in the National Treatment obligation and the Chapeau is not only the additional qualification of arbitrariness or lack of justification, but is also a difference of "nature and quality" of the discrimination. We respectfully submit that the first "difference" is judicial window-dressing, and that the second one can be equated with the necessity test. As for the first "difference," the Appellate Body does not provide any guidance as to how these forms of discrimination may differ in nature and quality.

---

[36] Appellate Body report on *United States—Standards for Reformulated and Conventional Gasoline* (WT/DS2/AB/R, adopted 20 May 1996), p. 22.

[37] Appellate Body report on *United States—Import Prohibition of Certain Shrimp and Shrimp Products* (WT/DS58/AB/R, adopted 6 November 1998), para. 40.

Nothing in its findings in the factual context of either *United States—Gasoline* or *United States—Shrimp–Turtle* provides support for such a view. In *United States—Gasoline*, it simply concludes that the US' omission to (1) explore adequately means of mitigating the administrative problems relied on as justification by the US for rejecting individual baselines for foreign refiners, and (2) count the costs for foreign refiners that would result from the imposition of statutory baselines "go well beyond what was necessary for the panel to determine that a violation of Article III:4 had occurred in the first place," and that "[t]he resulting discrimination must have been foreseen, and was not merely inadvertent or unavoidable."[38] If it is to be inferred from this that the difference in quality and nature between the two discrimination standards is the foreseeable and not merely inadvertent or unavoidable character of the discrimination, then it perfectly overlaps with the second "difference:" Avoidable discrimination and arbitrary or unjustifiable discrimination are one and the same standard. A discriminatory measure is unjustifiable and arbitrary when it could be avoided and it surely is not merely unavoidable when it is unjustifiable and arbitrary.

But this second "difference" is nothing new either. As amply demonstrated by the Appellate Body's reasoning in *United States—Gasoline*, the denominator common to all these qualifiers is a necessity test: a measure is avoidable because unnecessary; a measure can not be justified because less restrictive means were available. To quote Alan Sykes:

> This principle [of least restrictive means] is arguably more important than any other. In fact, one might argue that most of the important principles of policed decentralisation are corollaries of the least restrictive means principle. [. . .] A "disguised restriction" on trade is, by definition, not the least restrictive way to achieve a legitimate policy objective.[39]

And this is not just theory: in its appraisal of the Gasoline Rule's justification under the Chapeau, the Appellate Body relied on the panel's finding regarding the necessity of the Rule under Article XX(b), to support its finding that the discrimination was unjustifiable and arbitrary.[40] Concretely, it put forward the US' omission to use available verification and assessment techniques with regard to data relating to imported goods, on the basis of which the panel had found the measure already unnecessary under Article XX(b), as a ground for its finding that the

---

[38] Appellate Body report on *United States—Standards for Reformulated and Conventional Gasoline, supra* n. 36, p. 28.

[39] Alan Sykes, *Product Standards for Internationally Integrated Goods Markets* (1995) 118.

[40] Appellate Body report on *United States—Standards for Reformulated and Conventional Gasoline, supra* n. 36, p. 24–26, verbatim quoting from the panel report, paras. 6.26–6.28.

measure constituted an unjustifiable discrimination. Several authors, as well as a recent WTO panel,[41] appear to share this view:

> The Appellate Body imported a legal analysis more suitable to the paragraphs of Article XX when it dealt with the chapeau. In the course of interpreting the chapeau, the Appellate Body noted that the US had had more than one alternative measure whose use may have avoided any discrimination. Surprisingly, this test, which is often cited as "least restrictive" test, is the core of the necessity test usually reserved for an analysis of paragraphs (a), (b) and (d) of Art. XX. In this sense, one might argue that that the Appellate Body replaced its interpretation of "arbitrary," "unjustifiable" and "disguised" with an interpretation of necessary. [. . .] [I]f a necessity test were applied to both paragraphs (a), (b) and (d) of Art. XX and the chapeau, the chapeau would be rendered redundant.[42]

Thus, if a domestic regulation is challenged on discrimination grounds, and tentatively justified on the basis of a policy objective which requires a necessity connector, then the two-pronged Article XX test is in fact reduced to one: the discrimination must have been necessary.

The Appellate Body has also tried to distinguish the chapeau from the substance of Article III by emphasising the term "applied" in the chapeau, inferring from it that what is at issue here is not the discriminatory character of the regulation as such, but, rather, its *application*.[43] There are at least two arguments which seriously affect the credibility of this theory.

First, as discussed, to the extent that the Appellate Body appears to use now and then its Article III analysis to support its chapeau findings (such as in *US—Gasoline*), its theory does not correspond to its practice. Second, the Appellate Body has taken this position because it opines that doing otherwise would void the chapeau of all meaning. However, it is this very argument which makes acceptance of its theory rather difficult: if the chapeau of Article XX is concerned with discriminatory application of domestic regulation, Article X:3(a) would, to great extent, become "void of meaning." After all, Article X:3(a) requires Members to "administer in a uniform, impartial and reasonable manner all its laws, regulations, decisions and rulings" affecting, *inter alia*, the sale, distribution

---

[41] See footnote 355 of the panel report on *Korea—Measures Affecting Imports of Fresh, Chilled and Frozen Beef* (WT/DS161/R, WT/DS169/R, adopted 10 January 2001).

[42] Sung-Joon Cho, *Case Note*, retrievable at the European Journal of International Law website, www.ejil.org, at p. 10–11. Along the same lines, see Jeffrey Waincymer, "Reformulated Gasoline under Reformulated WTO Dispute Settlement Procedures: Pulling Pandora out of a Chapeau?", 18 *Michigan Journal of International Law* (1996) 141, 175.

[43] See the Appellate Body reports on *United States—Standards for Reformulated and Conventional Gasoline, supra* n. 36 (at p.25), and on *United States—Import Prohibition of Certain Shrimp and Shrimp Products, supra* n. 37 (para. 115), and the panel report on *European Communities—Measures Affecting Asbestos and Asbestos-Containing Products* (WT/DS135/R, adopted 5 April 2001) (at para. 8.226).

and processing of imports. One has difficulty defining the difference between an obligation to *administer* regulation in an impartial and uniform manner, on the one hand, and an obligation to *apply* regulation in a non-discriminatory manner, on the other hand.[44] Interestingly, then, the Appellate Body in *US—Shrimp* recognised this, *ex officio*, in the context of its chapeau analysis, stating that the US measures were "all contrary to the spirit, if not the letter, of Article X:3", which "bear[s] upon this matter," and found *"accordingly*, that the US measure is applied in a manner which amounts to a means not just of unjustifiable discrimination, but also of "arbitrary discrimination" [. . .] contrary to the requirements of the chapeau of Article XX."[45] One has difficulty understanding why the effectiveness theory would be an obstacle to equating Article III and the chapeau of Article XX if this does apparently not prevent the Appellate Body from equating Article X:3 with the chapeau. The same argument applies to Article III, at least as regards the second sentence of its second paragraph: the Appellate Body has repeatedly stated that this provision also deals with the discriminatory manner in which the measure is *applied*, and not the measure as such.[46] No wonder, then, that the recent panel Report in *EC-Asbestos* has proposed to apply the protective application theory of Article III:2, second sentence, to the chapeau of Article XX!

One may wish to reject this logic-dictated implosion of the seemingly sophisticated cascade of judicial interpretations under Article XX as simplistic rather than common sense. None the less, below, we will courageously[47] take this provocation one final step further, arguing that discrimination and necessity are also one and the same standard.

---

[44] As a matter of fact, the Appellate Body had exactly tried to distinguish Art. X:3(a) from Art. III by clarifying that the former "applies to the *administration* of laws, regulations, decisions and rulings," and that, "[t]o the extent that the laws, regulations, decisions and rulings themselves are discriminatory, they can be examined for their consistency with the relevant provisions of the GATT 1994." Appellate Body report on *EC—Regime for the Importation, Sale and Distribution of Bananas* (WT/DS27/AB/R, adopted 25 September 1997), para. 200.

[45] Appellate Body report on *United States—Import Prohibition of Certain Shrimp and Shrimp Products, supra* n. 37, paras. 182–183. Emphasis added.

[46] See, for instance, the Appellate Body report on *Japan—Taxes on Alcoholic Beverages, supra* n. 10, at p. 27.

[47] Perhaps not that courageously, considering Alan Sykes' observation in 1995 that "[d]iscriminatory measures achieve policy objectives, if at all, only in a manner that usually distorts trade unnecessarily, and thus are not least restrictive." Alan Sykes, *Product Standards for Internationally Integrated Goods Markets* 118 (1995). Or, similarly, Joel Trachtman, "Trade and . . . Problems, Cost-Benefit Analysis and Subsidiarity", 9 *European Journal of International Law* (1998) 32, 66: "Often, National Treatment examinations shade into simple means-end rationality testing, proportionality testing, necessity testing, balancing and cost-benefit analysis. [. . .] While rules of non-discrimination, such as National Treatment, are different from proportionality testing, balancing and cost-benefit analysis, they may under certain factual circumstances shade into a similar analysis."

(c)   The Relationship National Treatment—Non-Violation Complaints

Commentators have observed that non-violation cases in the past have played a pragmatic role of filling in the gap left by the general obligations in the GATT, including the Article III (national treatment) obligations.[48] Although Article XXIII:1(b) talks about "any measure, *whether or not* it conflicts with the provisions of this Agreement," and despite sporadic mingling of the two concepts by complainants in the past,[49] the only meaningful interpretation of Article XXIII must be that violation and non-violation are *mutually exclusive* concepts.[50] This seemingly straightforward conclusion is also confirmed by GATS Article XXIII which only distinguishes between a Member's failure to carry out its obligations (first paragraph) and measures which do not conflict with the provisions of the GATS (second paragraph).

The compelling logic of this conclusion should not guise its potential importance to our analysis of the scope of National Treatment in WTO law. In the present state of affairs, the wider we define the scope of National Treatment, the smaller becomes the potential coverage of the non-violation remedy, and *vice versa*. The findings in *Japan—Film* may in this respect provide important guidance to future panels dealing with facially origin-neutral measures. We submit that they have closed, to considerable extent, the gap between the substantive components making up violation and non-violation complaints. First, by finding that the nullification or impairment standard is the same for both violation and non-violation complaints (i.e. upsetting competitive relationship), the panel effectively ruled that the first component for finding a breach of National Treatment is the same as the one for finding non-violation: the measure must have adverse effects on the competitive conditions of foreign products. Second, and more importantly, the panel has not only implicitly but surely stated that an origin-neutral measure can only be shown to have caused non-violation nullification and impairment if it can be shown to be, at least, *de facto* discriminatory. It has, in addition,

[48] Sung-Joon Cho, *supra* n. 42, at 318.
[49] *Ibid.*, at 322, reporting that "there has been no prominent distinction between violation and non-violation complaints," and that non-violation complaints have "played an auxiliary role as a precaution against the failure to win the first violation argument."
[50] See also the panel report on *EEC—Payments and Subsidies Paid to Processors and Producers of Oilseeds and Related Animal-Feed Proteins* (L/6627, adopted 25 January 1990, BISD 37S/86). In this case, the panel, after having found a violation of GATT Art. III:4, examined whether this finding might make an examination of the question of the nullification or impairment of the tariff concessions—a non-violation complaint—unnecessary. The panel noted that *this would be the case if compliance by the Community with the finding on Art. III:4 would necessarily remove the basis of the United States claim of nullification or impairment.* It concluded that compliance with the finding on Art. III:4 could, but would not necessarily, eliminate the basis of the United States complaint that the benefits accruing to the Community producers of oilseeds impair the Community's tariff concessions for oilseeds. The panel therefore decided that it had to examine that complaint as well.

considered that the same criteria used in Article III:4 case law to make an affirmative finding of *de facto* discrimination are to be applied to non-violation analysis of origin-neutral measures,[51] and, conversely, has based its negative finding as regards discrimination under Article III:4 on its conclusions reached in that respect under Article XXIII:1(b).

It is remarkable that this holding has gone apparently unnoticed by commentators.[52] It basically says: origin-neutral measures must adversely affect competitive conditions and they must be *de facto* discriminatory for both violation and non-violation purposes. Put another way, for an origin-neutral measure to qualify for non-violation, it must first constitute a violation of National Treatment. Having regard to the remaining substantive and procedural differences between the two tracks rendering non-violation litigation more burdensome,[53] there would seem to be no use in using the non-violation venue to challenge origin-neutral measures. More fundamentally, the holding seems intellectually flawed: a measure can not at the same time be consistent and inconsistent with the agreements. Once a measure is found to be *de facto* discriminatory, any claim relating to it should be considered under Article III:4 rather than XXIII:1(b). This would suggest that the panel has failed to give a meaningful interpretation to either GATT Article III:4 or XXIII:1(b), or both. The Appellate Body in *EC—Asbestos*, however, appears to have approved of this approach, although it clarified that "[o]f course, if a measure 'conflicts' with a provision of the GATT 1994, that measure must actually fall within the scope of application of that provision of the GATT 1994."[54]

We submit that the *Japan—Film* panel's reasoning reflects the confusion which earlier panel and Appellate Body reports have created as

---

[51] One can only wonder to what extent the panel has contradicted itself in this respect by holding that, whereas the Appellate Body has rejected any role for regulatory intent in *de facto* discrimination determinations, reliance on intent as a means to support a non-violation claim should not be ruled out.

[52] See, for instance, James Durling and Simon Lester, "Original Meanings and the Film Dispute: The Drafting History, Textual Evolution, and Application of the Non-Violation Nullification and Impairment Remedy", 32 *George Washington Journal of International Law* (1999) 211. Norio Komuro, "Kodak-Fuji Film Dispute and the WTO Panel Ruling", 32 *Journal of World Trade* 161 (1998). Sara Dillon, "Fuji-Kodak, the WTO, and the Death of Domestic Political Constituencies", 8 *Minnesota Journal of Global Trade* (1999) 197.

[53] These are mainly:
—For a measure to be the subject matter of a non-violation complaint, the complainant must show that it had not anticipated the measure at the time concessions were scheduled nor could reasonably be expected to have done so. This requirement does of course not apply to measures subject of a violation complaint.
—Whereas a violation is considered *prima facie* to constitute a case of nullification or impairment pursuant to Art. 3.8 DSU—a rebuttable presumption—a member bringing a non-violation complaint must show—by means of "a detailed justification" (Art. 26 DSU) that the measure at hand has made more than a *de minimis* contribution to nullification and impairment.

[54] Appellate Body report, para. 187.

regards the scope of the National Treatment obligation. When one defines *de facto* discrimination exclusively in terms of a measure's adverse effects, and non-violation complaints require the same adverse effects to be shown, violation and non-violation will inevitably overlap. The panel was right in ruling that the Article III:4 *de facto* discrimination test advocated by recent Panels was, in addition to the specific requirements for non-violation, the correct test under Article XXIII:1(b): the simple existence of adverse effects. It erred, however, in basing its finding under Article III:4 on its non-violation analysis. *De facto discrimination should stop where non-violation begins.* For a Vienna Convention-conforming meaningful interpretation to be given to both provisions, it is necessary that the scope of the National Treatment obligation is more strictly circumscribed. Doing otherwise, as the *Japan—Film* panel has regrettably done—would render Article XXIII:1(b) void of all meaning.

2. The Advantages of Adding Some Rule to the Standard

In the light of these considerations, we posit that an integrated necessity test would allow us to more clearly map a boundary in WTO law between *de facto* discrimination and deregulation, and can to some extent be relied upon *ex ante*. This argument basically favours an increase of the rule-content in the standard of non-discrimination.[55] As we will show, however, it will not fundamentally change the nature of non-discrimination analysis, which will continue to present important characteristics of a standard. Rather, it attempts to relocate the exercise of judicial discretion from a totally unpredictable track to a somewhat more transparent and predictable one, hence reducing but not quashing, the discretionary margin.

Nevertheless, using Kaplow's definition of rules and standards in which the only distinction between rules and standards is the extent to which efforts to give content to the law are undertaken before or after individuals act,[56] the non-discrimination analysis by panels or the Appellate Body will undeniably be shifted towards the rule-side of the spectrum. we therefore need to explain why such a shift is desirable. We see the following advantages of adding some rule to the standard of current National Treatment analysis.

---

[55] National Treatment is somewhat hybrid: it presents characteristics of both rule and standard. As currently applied, however, it is certainly situated at the standard end of the spectrum. See Joel Trachtman, "Trade and . . . Problems, Cost-Benefit Analysis and Subsidiarity", 9 *European Journal of International Law* (1998) 32, 66: "National Treatment seems like a rule, but is often operated as a standard." For some general "rules versus standards" literature, see Louis Kaplow, "Rules versus Standards: An Economic Analysis", 42 *Duke Law Journal* (1992) 557; Pierre Schlag, "Rules and Standards", 33 *UCLA Law Review* (1985) 379.

[56] Louis Kaplow, *supra* n. 55, at 559.

(a) Predictability

This would be the most obvious and foremost benefit of adding rule to the standard. As evidenced by the above survey of inconsistencies, the WTO dispute settlement organs have not made sufficient efforts to make their analysis predictable or transparent. Although it is impossible, and wholly undesirable, to reduce judicial discretion in National Treatment analysis to zero, it would reduce transaction costs if this judicial determination itself would become more predictable. To clarify this, it is helpful to recall the distinction, which Trachtman has referred to in a recent article, between "primary predictability" and "secondary predictability."[57] Rules can enhance the ability of persons subject to the law to be able to plan and conform their conduct *ex ante* (primary predictability), but they can also do so *ex post*, after the conduct has taken place, allowing them to predict the outcome of dispute resolution (secondary predictability). The more rule-oriented non-discrimination test which we will suggest hereafter aims in particular at enhancing this secondary predictability.[58]

(b) Transparency and Legitimacy

Bob Hudec has fiercely criticised the Appellate Body's refusal to bring into the big wide open the reasoning which supposedly underlies its decisions with respect to likeness and regulatory intent.[59] Although we do not share his view that regulatory intent and likeness are or should be the cornerstone of National Treatment analysis, we do concur with his view that current case law evidences a lack of transparency. As a former deputy director in Korea's Ministry of Foreign Affairs and Trade, writing in his personal capacity, has put it:

> [The] coherent interpretation of "like" or "directly competitive or substitutable" products in the GATT is one of the most important issues with regard to the "judicialization" process of the WTO dispute settlement system. [. . .] [B]y applying the marketplace-oriented economic analysis in like product cases, WTO panels can enhance consistency among cases as well as trans-

---

[57] Joel Trachtman, "The Domain of WTO Dispute Resolution", 40 *Harvard International Law Journal* (1999) 333, 352.

[58] But see Wouter Wils, "The Search for the Rule in Art. 30 EEC: Much Ado About Nothing?", *European Law Review* (1993) 475, 489. This author has applied the standards vs. rules paradigm along the same lines to the ECJ's case law on Art. 28 EC Treaty, but concluded that return to a rule-based test was not necessarily warranted by enhanced predictability.

[59] Robert Hudec, *supra*, at 635: "One can see that the architects of the "aims and effects" approach were not really trying to change the underlying criteria of decision in these cases. Instead they were simply trying to bring this covert analysis into the open, where, supposedly, the quality of decision is improved because the parties are given the opportunity to address the real criteria of decision openly. The real meaning of the negative response of the Appellate Body is simply that such transparency is not likely to occur for a while."

parency of the decision process, two foremost values in the process. This consistency and transparency will improve acceptability of the decisions rendered by the dispute settlement bodies, which is the ultimate goal of WTO dispute settlement procedure.[60]

Like domestic courts, panels have a formal obligation under the DSU to give reasons.[61] Although this is not *expressis verbis* provided with regard to the Appellate Body's decisions, it does not seem tenable to say that, therefore, it does not need to give reasons. As the survey in chapter three should have demonstrated, however, it turns out to be a trying exercise to identify a consistent and clear line of reasoning underlying the panel and Appellate Body decisions regarding National Treatment, legitimate policy exceptions and non-violation, which appear to have covered many different ranges on the spectrum in a five year period.

(c) Administrative Cost of Formulation

Rules are traditionally perceived as entailing higher formulation costs than standards.[62] Here, however, we are dealing with the choice between one standard which is more rule-oriented than another. The alternatives to the rule-oriented solution which we will suggest have all been presented as a function of the likeness issue, be it the textual approach, the aims-and-effect theory, the "protective application" theory or the accordion theory. From our detailed description of the likeness debate above, it is sufficiently clear that this continuous swinging of the judicial pendulum from one extreme to the other reflects the intrinsic difficulty to resolve the matter by focusing on likeness and regulatory intent. This difficulty can be equated with a high cost of formulation.[63] In addition, the EC experience teaches us that likeness does not need to be a stumbling block in National Treatment implementation.[64]

---

[60] Won Mog Choi, *Progressive Interpretation of the Concepts of "Like" and "Directly Competitive or Substitutable" Products in the GATT/WTO Agreement: The Likeness— Substitutability Problem of Goods*, unpublished S.J.D. Dissertation, 2001, Georgetown University Law Center (on file with the author), at 10–11.

[61] Art. 12.7 DSU requires a Panel to set out "the basic rationale" behind any findings that it makes.

[62] Joel Trachtman, "The Domain of WTO Dispute Resolution", 40 *Harvard International Law Journal* (1999) 333, 355.

[63] See also Joel Trachtman, "Trade and . . . Problems, Cost-Benefit Analysis and Subsidiarity", 9 *European Journal of International Law* (1998) 32, 66: "While [National Treatment] may seem at a face level to be extremely easy to administer, this will often not be the case as the 'like products' issue is a proxy for a judicial examination of the rationality of regulatory categories."

[64] In practice, only very rarely was the "comparableness" of two products or services an issue in the non-discrimination analysis of the ECJ under Arts. 28, 43 or 49 EC Treaty. See Koen Lenaerts, "L'Egalité de Traitement en Droit Communautaire. Un Principe Unique aux Apparences Multiples", 27 *Cahiers de Droit Europeen* (1991) 3, 9: "La distinction opérée par une réglementation est, en fait, neutre en termes d'analyse discrimination/non-discrimination. Elle n'a que 'l'apparence de discrimination' et c'est par une appréciation

(d) Economies of Scale

The dynamics of economic integration make an increased reliance in future dispute settlement on Articles III of GATT and XVII of GATS very likely. The cases of Articles 28, 43 and 49 of the EC Treaty provide an instructive precedent in this respect. As other trade barriers gradually fell, the possibility to challenge origin-neutral domestic regulation as *de facto* discriminatory had caused an immense boom in requests for preliminary rulings to the ECJ. In the case of Article 28, it even prompted the ECJ to partially reverse its *Cassis de Dijon* case law in its notorious *Keck and Mithouard* judgment, by its own admission "[i]n view of the increasing tendency of traders to invoke Article [28] of the Treaty as a means of challenging any rules whose effects is to limit their commercial freedom even where such rules are not aimed at products from other Member States [. . .]"[65] Although this evolution was certainly in part due to the direct effect of these treaty provisions,[65a] allowing individual traders to rely on them in domestic courts, the relatively recent surge in Article III disputes suggest a similar pattern is looming in WTO law.[66] This anticipated greater frequency of use seems to warrant enhanced rule-orientation, which is bound to create economies of scale with increasing frequency.

C. AN INTEGRATED NECESSITY TEST IS WARRANTED BY A VIENNA
CONVENTION-CONFORMING INTERPRETATION

1. Using Causation Theory to Dissect the "Ordinary Meaning" or "Common Sense Meaning" of National Treatment Provisions

As the Appellate Body has repeatedly stressed, the WTO Agreements need to be interpreted in accordance with the Vienna Convention on the Law of Treaties,[67] in particular its Articles 31 and 32. This implies in the

du caractère comparable ou différent des divers cas en cause qu'il faudra déterminer si cette distinction est prohibée ou si elle s'impose. [. . .]" Judge Lenaerts then goes on to point out, however, that: "[l]a nature comparable ou différente de cas traités distinctement dans le droit communautaire apparaît, dès lors, comme une donnée non totalement objectivable. *La question de savoir si la distinction instituée est pertinente pour atteindre l'objectif poursuivi est d'une importance décisive.*"

[65]   Cases C–267–68/91, [1993] ECR I–6097, para. 14.

[65a] We have argued elsewhere that private party access to the WTO dispute settlement system is not as virtual as some would make it appear to be. See Todd Friedbacher and Gaëtan Verhoosel, *Private Party Access to the WTO Dispute Settlement System: A Few Pragmatic Thoughts*, paper presented at the "Regulatory Framework of Globalisation" Conference, Barcelona, October 2001 (on file with the author).

[66]   Bob Hudec has noted that de facto discrimination only became a major concern relatively recently, considering the first *Japan—Alcohol* panel in 1987 the first time it was addressed in GATT dispute settlement. See Robert Hudec, *supra* n. 4, at 622.

[67]   (1969), 8 International Legal Materials 679.

first place that treaty terms have to be given their "ordinary meaning."[68] We have earlier observed that GATT Article III:1 should be read as informing all paragraphs of GATT Article III, and not just GATT Article III:2, second sentence. What is then the ordinary meaning of "shall not accord less favourable treatment so as to afford protection"? The ordinary meaning of "shall accord treatment not less favourable" is pretty straightforward: "accord" expresses causation, whereas "treatment not less favourable" implies the absence of adverse effects which are specific ("less") to the imported products/services/service suppliers. This interpretation simply confirms the working definition of "according not less favourable treatment" which we had adopted at the beginning of this book and which we have consistently used thereafter: the causation of adverse effects on imported products/foreign services/service suppliers.

But the question then is: what should we understand by "causing adverse effects"? Using simple causation theory, we will demonstrate that the concept of causation is, in fact, a function of a necessity test.

(a) Mackie's Causes and Conditions

As Hart and Honoré have succinctly put it in their seminal *Causation in the Law*, "very often consideration of the purpose of a legal rule will show that certain kinds of harm alleged to have been caused by a breach

---

[68] Art. 31 ("General rule of interpretation") reads,

"1. A treaty shall be interpreted in good faith in accordance with the ordinary meaning to be given to the terms of the treaty in their context and in the light of its object and purpose.

2. The context for the purpose of the interpretation of a treaty shall comprise, in addition to the text, including its preamble and annexes:

(a) any agreement relating to the treaty which was made between all the parties in connexion with the conclusion of the treaty;

(b) any instrument which was made by one or more parties in connexion with the conclusion of the treaty and accepted by the other parties as an instrument related to the treaty.

3. There shall be taken into account together with the context:

(a) any subsequent agreement between the parties regarding the interpretation of the treaty or the application of its provisions;

(b) any subsequent practice in the application of the treaty which establishes the agreement of the parties regarding its interpretation;

(c) any relevant rules of international law applicable in the relations between the parties.

4. A special meaning shall be given to a term if it is established that the parties so intended."

Art. 32 ("Supplementary means of interpretation") reads,

"Recourse may be had to supplementary means of interpretation, including the preparatory work of the treaty and the circumstances of its conclusion, in order to confirm the meaning resulting from the application of article 31, or to determine the meaning when the interpretation according to article 31:

(a) leaves the meaning ambiguous or obscure; or

(b) leads to a result which is manifestly absurd or unreasonable."

of the rule are altogether outside its scope, since it is obvious that the rule is not concerned to give protection against that sort of harm."[69]

Along these lines, one could intuitively fill in: National Treatment in WTO law does not protect against adverse effects on foreign products or services which are the result of—are caused by—mere regulatory heterogeneity as between States. This would be a feature of deregulation. To find discrimination, more is needed than the occurrence of adverse effects on foreign products or services as a result of the differences between origin-neutral domestic regulations in different jurisdictions. The question "what more?" has already been answered in the last sentences: discrimination incorporates the understanding that there is a causal link between the domestic regulation and the adverse effects, rather than between the simple juxtaposition of regulations and those effects. We will demonstrate that this causal link is only established when the domestic regulation is unnecessarily trade-restrictive, i.e. creates unnecessary adverse effects to reach its regulatory goal, and argue that no discrimination analysis can be performed without carrying out a necessity test.

For a theoretical framework underpinning this intuitive argument, we will use John Mackie's authoritative piece "Causes and Conditions."[70] In his paper, Mackie tried to dissect the "common sense notion" of causation. His theory can be summarised as follows. A "cause" is an *insufficient* but *necessary* part of a condition which is itself *unnecessary* but *sufficient* for the result. Mackie terms such a condition an INUS condition. For instance, when a short-circuit is said to have caused a fire in a house, it is neither necessary nor sufficient for that fire, since the fire might have been caused by a short-circuit elsewhere or the overturning of a lighted oil stove, and it would not have occurred in the absence of inflammable materials or the presence of a suitably placed sprinkler. The short-circuit is a necessary part of a minimal sufficient condition of the fire. It is an INUS condition, or common sense cause. He speaks of a "minimal" sufficient condition to indicate that other such complex conditions may also have been a sufficient condition. The disjunction of all these minimal sufficient conditions constitutes a necessary and sufficient condition. In addition, the validity of this premise may be limited to a certain "field:" a short-circuit can only cause a fire in houses provided with electricity.

When the INUS condition is presented as "A", the other parts making up, jointly with A, the minimal sufficient condition as "X", the other minimal sufficient conditions as "Y", the field as "F", and the result as "P", the INUS condition can be defined as follows:

---

[69] HLA Hart and AM Honore, *Causation in the Law* (1959) 103.
[70] First published in 4 *American Philosophical Quarterly* (1965) 245, and reprinted as Chapter I in Ernest Sosa and Michael Tooley (eds.) *Causation* (OUP, 1993) 33.

A is an INUS condition of a result P in F if and only if, for some X and for some Y, (AX or Y) is a necessary and sufficient condition of P, but A is not a sufficient condition of P and X is not a sufficient condition of P.

(b) Applying Mackie's Formula to National Treatment

When we apply the formula to a case of alleged discrimination by domestic regulation against foreign products or services, we end up with the following:

If

$DR^{(1,2,3,4,\ldots,n)}$ =a domestic regulation which is a sufficient condition to bring about the achievement of a regulatory objective;

FR^x =the foreign regulations pursuing the same regulatory objective in different jurisdictions;

AE =the specific adverse effects suffered only by foreign goods or services;

F =the jurisdiction of $DR^{(1,2,3,4,\ldots,n)}$, i.e. where the AE occur

Then

DR^1 is a cause (or INUS condition) of AE in F if and only if, for some FR^x, (DR^1 FR^x) is a necessary and sufficient condition of AE, but DR^1 nor FR^x are individually sufficient conditions of AE. (1)

And

DR^1 is not a cause (or INUS condition) of AE in F if and only if, for some FR^x, (DR^1 FR^x) is not a necessary and sufficient condition of AE. (2)

Now here is the clue: DR^1 can only be a necessary part of a minimal sufficient condition (DR^1 FR^x), and hence an INUS condition or cause of AE, if it can not be replaced by DR^n as a necessary part of that minimal sufficient condition with FR^x, and hence an INUS condition or cause of AE. Or: when all other DR^n achieving the regulatory objective could be a "necessary" part of the sufficient condition, DR^1 could not be considered "necessary" because the sufficiency of (DR^1 FR^x) could be perfectly well assured by any other DR^n. Yet, if no other DR^n achieving the regulatory goal is capable of assuring the sufficiency of (DR^1 FR^x), DR^1 is considered "necessary." Or, in layman's words, the domestic regulation at hand can only be considered the cause of the adverse effects if another domestic regulation achieving the same regulatory objective can be found which, in conjunction with the foreign regulation, would not cause the same adverse effects. We can formalise this deduction as follows:

Therefore

DR^1 is a cause (or INUS condition) of AE in F if and only if, for some FR^x, (DR^n FR^x) is not a necessary and sufficient condition of AE. (3)

Premise (3) implies that a determination of whether or not a domestic regulation is discriminatory, i.e. has caused adverse effects for foreign products/services, involves, *ipso facto*, an investigation into the possibility of a less restrictive means to achieve the regulatory objective. A "least restrictive means" test is *inherent to* a causation, and hence, discrimination, determination. It is impossible to qualify a domestic regulation as discriminatory or not unless and until one has ran a counterfactual against the possibility of less restrictive alternatives. As demonstrated above, this follows inevitably from the commands of logic and causation theory. One can not overstate the importance of this conclusion: *regulation is de facto discriminatory to the extent it is unnecessary*. The adverse effects of a domestic regulation that goes beyond what is necessary to achieve the regulatory objective are not caused by the simple juxtaposition of jurisdictions. They are caused by the portion of the domestic regulation which is unnecessary to achieve the objective.

This is the distinction between non-discrimination and negative harmonisation: outlawing domestic regulations because they produce, in conjunction with foreign counterparts, adverse effects on foreign products/ services, would amount to negative harmonisation. Outlawing domestic regulations because they produce adverse effects on foreign products/ services not caused by the simple juxtaposition of jurisdictions, is non-discrimination. As we will further see, outlawing domestic regulations because they unnecessarily restrict imports and domestic production *alike*, is a form of deregulation.

The careful reader will have noted that in our formula, we accepted three factors as given: these are (1) the existence of adverse effects on the competitive conditions of foreign products/services; (2) the prima facie legitimacy of a regulatory objective and (3) the sufficiency of a domestic regulation for the achievement of this objective. These variables should continue to make up the "standard-like" remainder of a judicial discrimination determination. Indeed, we argue that in WTO law the likeness issue should be reduced to a more mechanical test, leaving these three variables to form the only real playground for judges.

(c) Parenthesis: Equating Non-Discrimination with Necessity, Not EC with WTO

1. One Chicken Can Produce Two Eggs

During the review of an earlier draft of this book, some of our readers at this point had made the observation that our theory boiled down to introducing a *Cassis de Dijon*-style construction in WTO law. And that they viewed this with certain scepticism, since the community of States gathering in Brussels is both qualitatively and quantitatively quite different from those gathering in Geneva. Now, we could not more wholeheartedly agree with them that, generally, the deep integration project of the EC is of course something quite different from what the WTO aspires to. And we have clearly stated so in chapter one of this book. Should we be doing what they fear we are, the validity of our thesis would indeed be seriously affected by its underlying premises. However, we are not cutting and pasting constructs from EC into WTO. Rather, we have developed, and further on will continue to develop, a number of arguments in support of our thesis which have not been inspired by the ECJ interpretation of the EC Treaty freedom provisions, but which draw from the specific function and provisions of the WTO.

Now, it is true that the resulting interpretation that we propose with regard to GATT and GATS National Treatment provisions bears "remarkable" resemblance to the one which has been developed in relation to the EC free movement provisions. It is, therefore, important to demonstrate that the basic underlying premise is not the egg produced by the EC chicken and subsequently added to the basket of the WTO chicken, but that it is the chicken which is able to produce both the WTO and EC eggs. Or put another way, we submit that causation is a constitutive element of both WTO National Treatment and EC Freedom provisions, and that it is this common element which explains how one can arrive at a relatively similar interpretative construction of these different provisions. Indeed, when one opens an authoritative textbook on EC law, it can typically be read that the freedom concept used in the EC Treaty has been interpreted as not simply requiring non-discrimination, but also prohibiting equally applicable trade-restrictive measures, the latter traditionally being depicted as a discipline which reaches qualitatively further into domestic regulatory systems than the former.[71] In this section, we intend to demonstrate that this widely shared perception of ECJ case law on free movement of goods and services and freedom of establishment as going beyond non-discrimination, is, at least partially, misguided in the light of a proper causation analysis. Instead, we posit, what so often has been considered "negative harmonisation" or "deregulation" is merely a process directed at the abolishment of more subtle forms of *de facto* discrimination, with the exception of a few isolated cases.

2. Trade in Goods

The saga surrounding Article 28 is both well-known and well-documented.[72] One shall recall that the ECJ had ruled in *Dassonville* that all trading rules enacted by member states which are capable of hindering, directly or indirectly, actually or potentially, intra- community trade are to

---

[71] PJG Kapteyn and P Verloren van Themaat, *Introduction to the Law of the European Communities* 584 (1998). See also Piet Eeckhout, "The EC Response", paper presented at the World Trade Forum 2000 conference *The Role of the Judge: Lessons for the WTO* (on file with the author), at 84.

[72] For a detailed survey, see Peter Oliver, *Free Movement of Goods in the European Community* (1996).

be considered as measures having an effect equivalent to quantitative restrictions.[73] Equally well-known, the *Cassis de Dijon* judgment subsequently read that obstacles to movement within the community resulting from disparities between the national laws relating to the marketing of the products in question must be accepted in so far as those provisions may be recognised as being necessary in order to satisfy mandatory requirements.[74] And finally, in *Keck and Mithouard*, the ECJ was said to have partially reversed its prior case law, stating that the application to products from other Member States of national provisions restricting or prohibiting certain selling arrangements is not such as to hinder directly or indirectly, actually or potentially, trade between Member States within the meaning of the *Dassonville* judgment, so long as those provisions apply to all relevant traders operating within the national territory and so long as they affect in the same manner, in law and in fact, the marketing of domestic products and of those from other Member States.[75]

Much of the immense confusion following the *Cassis de Dijon* and *Keck and Mithouard* case law has to do with semantics. The language of the ECJ in its dealing with Article 28 claims has varied considerably, and has not rarely skirted the borderline of contradiction and inconsistency. However, when one looks at the facts of those cases, and one applies the above proposed causation-based definition of discrimination, it becomes readily apparent, we argue, that the ECJ has crossed the line of deregulation only in a limited number of cases between the *Cassis de Dijon* and *Keck and Mithouard* judgments. Starting with the holding of *Cassis de Dijon*, it perfectly reflects a causation-based discrimination test: it says that the differences resulting from the juxtaposition of domestic origin-neutral regulatory frameworks can not result in a breach of Article 28 as long as the domestic regulation at issue produces the least adverse effects possible to achieve the regulatory objective. Although it was clear from the facts of the case that the measure at hand adversely affected foreign products more than domestic, the Court did not specify that this was a requirement for a domestic regulation to be caught by Article 28. Although in its subsequent case law the Court has nevertheless often required a domestic regulation to adversely affect foreign products more than domestic ones for it to fall within the scope of Article 28,[76] it departed from that practice in a limited number of rulings, prominent examples of which are *Cinéthèque*[77] and *Milk Substitutes*.[78] Both cases

---

[73] Case 8/74, [1974] ECR 837, para. 5.
[74] Case 120/78, [1979] ECR 649, para. 8.
[75] Cases C–267–8/91, [1993] ECR I–6097, para. 16.
[76] For copious reference to such case law, see Lucette Defalque, "Le Concept de Discrimination en Matière de Libre Circulation des Marchandises", *Cahiers de droit Europeen* 471, 477 (1987).
[77] Case 60–1/84, [1985] ECR 2605.
[78] Case 216/84, [1988] ECR 793.

concerned a domestic prohibition which clearly affected domestic and foreign products in the same manner. By not requiring the showing of greater adverse effects on foreign products than on domestic ones, the Court omitted the first step in any discrimination analysis, which is to compare the relative situations of domestic and foreign products, thereby entering the realm of deregulation.

The Court has had particular problems in applying this requirement of adverse effects in a consistent manner to cases involving domestic regulations restricting the circumstances in which products may be marketed. In some cases the Court did require that imports were more adversely affected than domestic production. For example, it held in *Oebel*[79] that trade between Member States was not restricted, within the meaning of that provision, by legislation which prohibited the delivery of bakery wares to retailers between certain hours, since deliveries to wholesalers were permitted. In *Blesgen*[80] the Court held that a prohibition on the sale of strong alcoholic beverages in bars and restaurants was not of such a nature as to impede trade between Member States, and in *Quietlynn*[81] it reached a similar conclusion with regard to a law prohibiting the sale of pornography except in licensed "sex shops."

During that same period, however, the Court has regularly interpreted the scope of Article 28 as not requiring in such cases the showing of greater adverse effects on imports than on domestic production. The first such case, *Oosthoek*,[82] concerned a Netherlands law which prohibited the offering or giving of products as free gifts within the framework of a commercial activity. The Court held that:

> Legislation which restricts or prohibits certain forms of advertising and certain means of sales promotion may, although it does not directly affect imports, be such as to restrict their volume because it affects marketing opportunities for the imported products. The possibility cannot be ruled out that to compel a producer either to adopt advertising or sales promotion schemes which differ from one Member State to another or to discontinue a scheme which he considers to be particularly effective may constitute an obstacle to imports even if the legislation in question applies to domestic products and imported products without distinction.

The regulation at hand clearly adversely affected the competitive conditions of imports and domestic products alike. A similar approach was adopted in *Buet*[83] and *Aragonesa de Publicidad.*[84]

---

[79] Case 155/80, [1981] ECR 1993.
[80] Case 75/81, [1982] ECR 1211.
[81] Case C–23/89, [1990] ECR I–3095.
[82] Case 286/81, [1982] ECR 4575.
[83] Case 382/87, [1989] ECR 1235.
[84] Joined Cases C–1/90 and C–176/90, [1991] ECR I–4151.

Marenco, writing in the aftermath of *Cassis de Dijon*, has forcefully opined that such omission of an imports-specific adverse effects requirement was contrary to the intention of the drafters of the treaty:

> [T]he purpose of the provisions of the Treaty is not to prohibit Member States' regulation as such, in order to achieve uniformity of these regulations by simply quashing them. These provisions are concerned with *the effects which those regulations specifically have on trade between Member states*, and not with the *general restrictive effect*, which is a feature of all regulation and which, by its very nature, generally affects private economic freedom. (original emphasis)
>
> [...]
>
> [T]he *prohibition* of Article [28] always presupposes *a greater disadvantage* for imports than for domestic production.[85] (original emphasis)

In addition, restrictions which by chance do affect more imported products but which result from the mere juxtaposition of regulatory jurisdictions, do not constitute discrimination in his view, because there is no causal link between the measure and the adverse effects: the cause is the concurrent existence of regulations. Nevertheless, he sees this causal link reestablished if the domestic regulation is not necessary to reach the purported objective.[86] This constitutes in his view simply a more subtle form of *de facto* discrimination, one which can only be discovered by assessing the relation between the regulation and its purported regulatory goal:

> Such discrimination can not be detected directly, since, by hypothesis, there is no difference between the situation of domestic production and that of

---

[85] Giuliano Marenco, "Pour une Interprétation Traditionelle de la Notion de Mesure d'Effet Equivalent à une Restriction Quantitative", *Cahiers de Droit Europeen* (1984) 291, 318. Translation by this author: "Selon cette optique, les règles du traité n'ont pas pour but, en revanche, d'interdire les réglementations des Etats membres en tant que telles, afin de parvenir à l'uniformité de ces réglementations par leur simple suppression. Ces règles se préoccupent des effets que ces réglementations exercent *de manière spécifique sur les échanges entre les Etats membres*, non pas de *l'effet restrictif général*, qui est propre à toute réglementation, du seul fait de son existence, et qui affecte, de manière générale, la liberté économique privée. [...] [Sa thèse] admet que *l'interdiction* visée à l'article [28] présuppose toujours *un désavantage plus grand* pour les importations que pour la production interne." Original emphasis.

[86] *Ibid.*, at 321, 323: "L'état est en principe libre de déterminer le contenu de ses règles. Il est des lors inévitable que ces règles diffèrent d'un état membre à l'autre. L'effet restrictif résulte des lors non pas du choix exercé nécessairement de manière individuelle, par chaque état, mais de la juxtaposition de ces choix. L'effet restrictif n'est pas plus imputable a la mesure de l'état d'importation qu'a celle de l'état d'exportation. Il n'y a aucun lien de causalité entre chaque choix individuel et les effets restrictifs. [...] Le lien de causalité entre la mesure et les effets restrictifs spécifiques est retabli, lorsque le choix effectué par l'état membre comporte des effets restrictifs qui vont au-dela de ce qui est rendu inevitable par le fait que la competence normale, se situant au niveau des états membres et non de la Communauté, engendre des réglementations différentes. Ce dépassement a lieu lorsque l'état prend des mesures qui ne répondent pas a un objectif digne de protection ou sont disproprtionnées par rapport a un tel objectif. Les effets plus onéreux de la mesure sur les importations par rapport a la production nationale sont dans ce cas a attribuer a une attitude discriminatoire tout au moins par negligence [...]"

imports, except for the fact that the latter is compelled to go through the adaptations required by the importing State. This discrimination can only be detected by assessing the regulation in relation to its objective.[87]

He concludes that *Cassis de Dijon*, and subsequent case law, when seen through this prism of causality-based discrimination, can all be explained in terms of non-discrimination. Although Marenco admittedly failed to explain the above case law which did go beyond non-discrimination, his analytical framework is clearly very close to the one we suggest to apply in the WTO framework.

The Court would eventually do justice to Marenco's vision. After a cascade of criticism that Article 28 was being "overstretched,"[88] the Court "clarified" its case law on Article 28 in *Keck and Mithouard*. In paragraph 16 of the judgment, the Court divided origin-neutral ("indistinctly applicable") domestic regulation in two categories for the purpose of Article 28:

—product requirements (such as requirements as to designation, form, size, weight, composition, presentation, labelling and packaging);
—national provisions restricting or prohibiting certain selling arrangements.

Whereas the first category remains subject to the *Cassis de Dijon* test, i.e. will pass the Article 28 test if they are necessary to reach the regulatory objective, the second henceforth "fall out of the scope of Article 28" if measures in this category apply to all affected traders operating within the national territory and they affect in the same manner, in law and in fact, the marketing of domestic products and of those from other Member States.

Although the judgment has been subjected to stinging criticism, and its wording is admittedly inadequate, there is definitely also merit to its rationale. It has brought Article 28 back within the lines of a causation-based non-discrimination test. First, the Court states that it wishes to clarify its case law because rules are increasingly being challenged "even where such rules are not aimed at products from other Member States."[89] This motivation for change strongly suggests that the import-specific adverse effects requirement is again part of Article 28 law: only if imports suffer more than domestic production, can Article 28 come into play. Second, this also explains the dichotomy operated by the Court: whereas "product requirements" are, by their very nature, likely to

---

[87] *Ibid.*, at 322. This author's translation: "Une telle discrimination ne peut être constatée directement, car par hypothèse il n'y a pas de différence entre la situation de la production interne et celle de la production importée à part la nécessité pour cette dernière de devoir se soumettre aux manipiulations requises par l'Etat membre de l'importation. Elle ne peut être décélée qu'en appréciant la mesure par rapport aux objectifs poursuivis."
[88] Peter Oliver, *supra* n. 72, at 96.
[89] Para. 15 of the judgment.

adversely affect imports more than domestic production (because they need to be adapted to a second set of regulations, contrary to the domestic product), "selling arrangements" are not (because they normally do not require anything more from imports than from domestic production).[90] The former remain therefore subject to a necessity test (if adverse effects can be shown), while the latter do not: only if they can be shown to be *de jure* or *de facto* discriminatory, can they be brought within Article 28 scrutiny. Advocate-General Van Gerven has interpreted this condition as meaning that a measure must be worded as being applicable without distinction ("in law"—*de jure*) and may not give rise, "in point of its effects," to unequal access to the market on the part of domestic and imported products ("in fact"—*de facto*).[91]

In conclusion, although it would have been preferable that the Court had adopted a causation-based discrimination test in terms more general than the very formalistic and rigid dichotomy of *Keck and Mithouard*, it has at least "brought into the open" the pattern implicitly underlying its previous case law and corrected the deregulatory excesses of some of them. Advocate-General Van Gerven sums it up just nicely:

> The question which arises therefore is [. . .] whether the Court intended to reduce the prohibition set out in Article [28] of the EC Treaty to a prohibition of discrimination (in a broad sense). [. . .] The question is perhaps not of very much significance, since—in so far as I have been able to make an overview of the case-law—the bulk, if not all of, the measures considered in the Court' s case-law, whether they were product requirements or requirements not relating to products applicable "without distinction," contained some form or other of "discrimination in fact," at least if this is understood as meaning any additional burden imposed by the measure when products are imported from other Member States.[92]

[90] See the conclusions of Advocate-General Van Gerven in *Boermans* (Case C–401–02/92): "Product requirements by nature impede access to the market of the Member State which laid them down, because they mean that a product lawfully manufactured and marketed in the Member State of origin must be adapted when it is imported into another Member State in order to suit the product requirements in force there, and therefore have the effect of requiring the product to satisfy the requirements of two different sets of legislation [. . .]. In view of the costs entailed by this when the product is imported, the producer has an additional burden imposed upon him, which almost certainly has the effect of impeding the imported product' s access to the market or even, where those costs are prohibitive, of making access impossible. This is not the case with legislation prohibiting or restricting sales promotion methods: such legislation does not normally mean that the imported products to which it applies have to be adapted in point of their intrinsic or extrinsic characteristics in order to satisfy the statutory requirements of the importing State (the fact that differing sales methods have to be used depending on the Member State concerned may admittedly also entail additional costs, but certainly to a lesser degree." *Ibid.*, para. 20.

[91] *Ibid.*, para. 23.

[92] *Ibid.*, para. 24. Compare with Piet Eeckhout, "After Keck and Mithouard: Free Movement of Goods in the EC, Market Access, and Non-Discrimination", in Thomas Cottier, Petros Mavroidis and Patrick Blatter (eds.) *Regulatory Barriers and the Principle of Non-Discrimination in World Trade Law* (2000) 203: "Although in relation to [selling arrangements] the language of non-discrimination is no longer used in the Court's case-law,

3. Freedom to Provide Services and Freedom of Establishment

As regards the freedom to provide services (Article 49) and the freedom of establishment (Article 43), the ECJ has roughly sailed the same course.[93] The ECJ transplanted its *Cassis de Dijon* language for the first time most prominently to Article 49 in *Säger*,[94] and to Article 43 in *Kraus*.[95] In *Säger* the Court held that Article 49 of the Treaty requires not only the elimination of all discrimination against a person providing services on the ground of his nationality but also the abolition of any restriction, even if it applies without distinction to national providers of services and to those of other Member States, when it is liable to prohibit or otherwise impede the activities of a provider of services established in another Member State where he lawfully provides similar services. It reiterated established case law,[96] according to which a Member State may not make the provision of services in its territory subject to compliance with all the conditions required for establishment and thereby deprive of all practical effectiveness Article 49. Such a restriction is all the less permissible where the service is supplied without its being necessary for the person providing it to visit the territory of the Member State where it is provided.[97] The freedom to provide services may be limited only by rules which are justified by imperative reasons relating to the public interest and which apply to all persons or undertakings pursuing an activity in the State of destination, in so far as that interest is not protected by the rules to which the person providing the services is subject in the Member State in which he is established. In particular, those requirements must be objectively necessary in order to ensure compliance with professional rules and to guarantee the protection of the recipient of services and they must not exceed what is necessary to attain those objectives.[98]

there remains scope for identifying elements of discrimination against imported products also in those cases."

[93] For a detailed survey from 1989 onwards, see Hugues Calvet and Franck Dintilhac, "Chronique de Jurisprudence en matière de Liberté d'Etablissement et de Libre prestation de Services", 27 *Revue Trimestrielle de Droit Europeen* (1991) 59, Jean Guy Huglo, "Chronique de Jurisprudence en matière de Liberté d'Etablissement et de Libre prestation de Services", 28 *Revue Trimestrielle de Droit Europeen* (1992) 687; Jean Guy Huglo, "Chronique de Jurisprudence en matière de Liberté d'Etablissement et de Libre prestation de Services", 29 *Revue Trimestrielle de Droit Europeen* (1993) 655; Jean Guy Huglo, "Chronique de Jurisprudence en matière de Liberté d'Etablissement et de Libre prestation de Services", 30 *Revue Trimestrielle de Droit Europeen* (1994) 465; Jean Guy Huglo, "Chronique de Jurisprudence en matière de Liberté d'Etablissement et de Libre prestation de Services", 31 *Revue Trimestrielle de Droit Europeen* (1995) 827; Jean Guy Huglo, "Chronique de Jurisprudence en matière de Liberté d'Etablissement et de Libre prestation de Services", 32 *Revue Trimestrielle de Droit Europeen* (1996) 741.

[94] Case C–76/90, [1991] ECR I–4221.
[95] Case C–19/92, [1993] ECR I–1663.
[96] See, for instance, Case C–340/89, [1991] ECR I–2357, para. 15.
[97] Paras. 12–13 of the judgment.
[98] Para. 15 of the judgment.

Similarly, in *Kraus* the Court held that Article 43 precludes any national measure governing the conditions under which an academic title obtained in another Member State may be used, where that measure, even though it is applicable without discrimination on grounds of nationality, is liable to hamper or to render less attractive the exercise by Community nationals of fundamental freedoms guaranteed by the Treaty. The situation would be different only if such a measure pursued a legitimate objective compatible with the Treaty and was justified by pressing reasons of public interest.[99]

Applying once more our causation gauge to this case law, we can see it is in principle perfectly compatible with a non-discrimination test as defined earlier: when the adverse effects on foreign services and service suppliers are caused not simply by the differences as between regulatory systems, for instance as regards professional qualification requirements, but by a regulation which, upon examination, turns out to be unnecessarily restrictive, the latter can rightfully said to be discriminatory using a causation test. But the question also arises here as to what extent the domestic regulation at hand needs to adversely affect foreign services and service suppliers more than domestic ones under this case law. Its language ("liable to prohibit or otherwise impede the activities of a provider of services established in another Member State", "liable to hamper or to render less attractive the exercise by Community nationals of fundamental freedoms guaranteed by the Treaty") seemed to suggest this requirement still stood. And indeed, most of the cases dealing with "indistinctly applicable" national measures regulating services or establishment concerned measures which were not overtly discriminatory, but had the effect of imposing "an unequal burden or a discriminatory effect of some kind, or a desire to protect some part of the domestic market from foreign competition."[100]

The Court's judgment in *Schindler*,[101] however, appeared to have chosen the *Cinéthèque* track in defining the scope of Article 49. It held that this provision also covers national legislation on lotteries which wholly precludes lottery operators from other Member States from promoting their lotteries and selling their tickets in the Member State which enacted that legislation. Such regulation obviously had the same adverse effects on domestic and foreign suppliers.

---

[99]   Para. 32 of the judgment.

[100]   Paul Craig and Gráinne de Búrca, *EC Law: Text, Cases and Materials* (1995) 775, endorsed by Walter van Gerven, "Articles 30, 48, 52 and 59 after *Keck and Mithouard*, and Protection of Rights arising from Directives after *Faccini Dori*", 2 *Columbia Journal of European Law* (1996) 217, 220. Marenco, not surprisingly, 8 years after his seminal piece on Art. 28, has vigorously defended the view that all of the Court's case law on services and establishment can be fitted into the non-discrimination straightjacket: Giuliano Marenco, "The Notion of Restriction on the Freedom of Establishment and Provision of Services in the Case Law of the Court", *Yearbook of European Law* (1992) 111.

[101]   Case C–275/92, [1994] ECR I–1039.

Following this perceived "overstretching" of Article 49, similarly to what happened in the Article 28 context, in *Alpine Investments*[102] it was argued that the Court should apply its *Keck and Mithouard* ruling to Article 49, and find that a general prohibition on financial intermediaries who offer investments in off-market commodities futures from "cold calling" potential clients, falls outside the scope of Article 49. It was submitted that the prohibition at issue fell outside the scope of Article 49 of the Treaty because it was a generally applicable measure, it was not discriminatory and neither its object nor its effect was to put the national market at an advantage over providers of services from other Member States. Since it affected only the way in which the services were offered, it was analogous to the non-discriminatory measures governing selling arrangements which, according to the decision in *Keck and Mithouard*, do not fall within the scope of Article 28 of the Treaty. The Court did not accept the argument:

> Although a prohibition such as the one at issue in the main proceedings is general and non-discriminatory *and neither its object nor its effect is to put the national market at an advantage over providers of services from other Member States*, it can none the less [. . .] constitute a restriction on the freedom to provide cross-border services. Such a prohibition is not analogous to the legislation concerning selling arrangements held in Keck and Mithouard to fall outside the scope of Article [28] of the Treaty. [. . .] A prohibition such as that at issue is imposed by the Member State in which the provider of services is established and affects not only offers made by him to addressees who are established in that State or move there in order to receive services but also offers made to potential recipients in another Member State. It therefore directly affects access to the market in services in the other Member States and is thus capable of hindering intra-Community trade in services.[103] (emphasis added)

We would concur with the opinion of the many commentators who, speculating about the exact impact of this ruling, find it impossible to draw any clear-cut conclusions from it.[104] On the one hand, the Court, in what seems to be a statement of principle, rejects the notion that foreign suppliers need to be more affected than domestic ones. On the other hand, it stated at the same time that a prohibition does not constitute a restriction on freedom to provide services within the meaning of Article 49 solely by virtue of the fact that other Member States apply less strict rules to providers of similar services established in their territory.[105] One

---

[102] Case C–384/93, [1995] ECR, I–1141.

[103] Paras. 35–38 of the judgment.

[104] See, for instance, Malcolm Ross, "Article 59 and the Marketing of Financial Services", *European Law Review* (1995) 507; Vassilis Hatzopoulos, "Comments on Alpine Investments", *Common Market Law Review* (1995) 1436; Geert Straetmans, "Case Note: Alpine Investments", 2 *Columbia Journal of European Law* (1996) 154.

[105] Para. 27 of the judgment.

can then only wonder how to reconcile these statements. An answer may perhaps be found in the factual particularities of the case: at issue was not the "import" of services, but the "export" of services. Thus, the domestic regulation was said to restrict outbound services trade, rather than inbound trade, by depriving the operators concerned of a "rapid and direct technique for marketing and for contacting potential clients in other Member States."[106]

In any case, the Court has certainly not shut the door to the application of *Keck and Mithouard*-like limitations in future Article 49 cases, merely noting that in this particular case, the regulation at issue was not analogous to a selling arrangement. This constitutes indeed an implicit admission that *Keck and Mithouard* may apply in other cases.[107]

To sum up, assuming that foreign service suppliers still need to be more adversely affected than domestic ones after *Schindler* and *Alpine Investments*, the domestic regulation of services which are provided cross-border (Article 49) or through establishment (Article 43) is subject to a causation-based non-discrimination test, as defined earlier. The Court has interpreted this test in its case law as:

—requiring different treatment of services supplied cross-border than otherwise like services supplied through establishment, in that the former can not be required to comply with all regulation applicable to the latter;
—requiring Member States to take into account the protection of the regulatory goal afforded by the regulatory system of the foreign supplier's home State—degree requirements, for instance, for foreign academic or professional qualifications—when applying their own domestic regulation.

Both aspects of the test are natural implications of a causation-based discrimination test: in both cases, the achievement of the regulatory goal does not require more than what the ECJ restricts Member States' autonomy to.

(d) Casting GATT/GATS National Treatment on a Causation Mould

What happens when we cast GATT/GATS National Treatment Analysis on such a causation mould? The case study of the EC has showed us that non-discrimination can degenerate into negative harmonisation or deregulation if either (1) it is no longer required that the competitive conditions of foreign products/services are specifically adversely affected, or

---

[106] Para. 28 of the judgment.
[107] Geert Straetmans, *supra* n. 104, at 159. But see Giuseppe Tesauro, "The Community's Internal market in the Light of the recent Case Law of the Court of Justice", *Yearbook of European Law* (1995) 1, 7, who takes the view that the *Keck*-extension to services "has in any event been ruled out by the Court" in *Alpine Investments*.

(2) when such specific adverse effects need not be caused by a domestic regulation, but may also flow from the simple juxtaposition of regulatory jurisdictions. In the WTO context, the first peril is not present: the adverse effects must always specifically concern foreign products/services. This was, to the extent necessary, confirmed by the panel in *Japan—Film*, when it rejected the US argument that the Large Stores Law was discriminatory, referring to the failure of such arguments with respect to Sunday Closing laws in the EC context.[108] It was subsequently explicitly reiterated by the Appellate Body in its report on *Korea—Beef.*[109] The only line which therefore needs to be drawn in WTO law between non-discrimination and deregulation is a function of a determination of the cause.

In such a causation-based discrimination analysis, the emphasis is shifted from likeness to the legitimacy of the regulatory objective and a generalised least restrictive means test. Likeness can be deflated to its original status, i.e. a basis of comparison. In both the cases of GATT and GATS, likeness should be based on cross-price elasticity. As explained above, the double advantage of such a shift lies in the resulting "*externalisation*" of judicial reasoning, on the one hand, and the "*objectification*" of the parameters they use, on the other. Panels and Appellate Body are no longer able to hide their real reasoning behind the likeness façade, and they have to apply criteria which are susceptible of a rational debate (legitimacy of the purported policy goal and necessity of the regulatory means employed). The third remaining element of judicial assessment is the finding of the existence of adverse effects: do some, most or all of the foreign products/services/service suppliers need to be affected to justify an affirmative finding? This question seems to have been answered by *Chile—Alcohol* as regards GATT: the panel found that the conditions of competition had been modified in favour of domestic production because over 95 per cent of the disadvantaged products were taxed at the highest rate, while roughly 75 per cent of domestic production would enjoy the lowest tax rate.[110] As regards GATS, the *EC—Bananas* panel found that the conditions of competition had been modified in favour of domestic wholesalers because over 90 per cent of the disadvantaged wholesalers were nationals of the complaining countries, while over 75 per cent of the advantaged wholesalers were nationals of the defending party.[111] One can

---

[108] Panel Report on *Japan—Measures Affecting Consumer Photographic Film and Paper* (WT/DS44/R, adopted 22 April 1998), para. 10.227.

[109] Appellate Body report on *Korea—Measures Affecting Imports of Fresh, Chilled and Frozen Beef* (WT/DS161/AB/R, WT/DS169/AB/R, adopted 10 January 2001), paras. 135–137.

[110] Panel Report on *Chile—Taxes on Alcoholic Beverages, supra* n. 3, para. 7.158.

[111] Panel report on *EC—Regime for the Importation, Sale and Distribution of Bananas, supra* n. 24, paras. 7.332–7.338. See also Robert Hudec, *supra* n. 4, at 640: "For all one can tell from the Panel opinion, the analysis of whether the regulation was discriminatory depended solely on a head count of the nationality of the affected suppliers, whatever the underlying reason for this distribution."

infer from these rulings that a "clear majority" of foreign products/ services/service suppliers must be affected.[112]

2. GATS Article XVII: Textual Support in Footnote 10

The Appellate Body has inferred from the absence of the phrase "so as to afford protection" in GATS Article XVII that Panels should not engage in a protective application test. Let us assume that this is a correct interpretation, and, consequently, that the phrase does not inform the National Treatment obligation under GATS. Does this mean that the simple causation of adverse effects on foreign services/service suppliers is sufficient to find a breach of National Treatment? We do not believe so, and argue that, independently from any reference to "so as to afford protection," there is a sound textual basis for reading a necessity test in GATS Article XVII. Indeed, footnote 10 to GATS Article XVII:1 provides,

> [s]pecific commitments assumed under this Article shall not be construed to require any Member to compensate for any inherent competitive disadvantages which result from the foreign character of the relevant services or service suppliers.

According to the New Shorter Oxford English Dictionary, "inherent" means "existing in something as an essential, permanent, or characteristic attribute or quality."[113] We infer from this that, when a regulation exists or is adopted in country X which is drafted in origin-neutral terms, and service suppliers of country Y argue that their competitive conditions are, as a result, adversely affected, we would not be able to strike down such a regulation as discriminatory if its adverse effects on foreign suppliers result inherently from their foreign character. We take this to mean that the foreign character and the measure constituted together the sufficient condition of the adverse effects, and that the latter must have been unavoidable, no matter what sort of measure was adopted to reach the same regulatory objective. Put another way, the concept of "foreign character" of a service or service supplier puts into play the causal link between the simple juxtaposition of regulatory jurisdictions and adverse effects on foreign services/service suppliers. It follows that the foreign character must be a necessary condition of the adverse results, whereas the regulation at hand must not: any regulation achieving the same regulatory objective could have constituted the necessary condition, the occurrence of

---

[112] For a detailed analysis of the distribution of adverse effects, see Lothar Ehring, "Non-Discrimination in WTO Law: National and Most-Favoured-Nation Treatment or Equal Treatment?", *Jean Monnet Seminar Paper*, Harvard University, 2001 (on file with the author), who distinguishes in this respect between a "diagonal" and an "asymmetric" approach.

[113] L Brown (ed.) *New Shorter Oxford English Dictionary* (Clarendon Press, 1993), 1368.

which forms together with the foreign character a sufficient cause for the adverse effects. A WTO panel or Appellate Body would thus need to embark on a *counterfactual* analysis to determine whether the adverse effects were caused by the foreign character or not.

This counterfactual could be run as follows. If the existing measure would be replaced by a measure different from the one in existence/adopted but still achieving the regulatory objective, would the adverse effects still have occurred? If different measures pursuing the same regulatory objective would have resulted in the same adverse effects, the measure is cleared, because inherently due to the foreign character of the service or service supplier. In that case, the regulation at hand was clearly not a necessary condition to bring about the observed adverse effect. It follows from this that a panel or the Appellate Body would actually need to conduct a "least restrictive means" analysis under Art XVII to determine whether adverse effects result inherently from the foreign character of service suppliers. Only if the adverse effects persist, regardless of the nature of the measure, could they be said to be inherent. Thus, if a less restrictive measure achieving the same objective can be shown to lead to less or no adverse effects, the more restrictive regulation can be stricken down as discriminatory regulation.

Example: the same high-standard professional qualification requirement is imposed on all service suppliers supplying services in country X. Foreign suppliers attack the regulation because they consider it *de facto* discriminatory. Country X argues, however, that any resulting adverse effect is inherent to the foreign character of these suppliers, including the lack of adequate training in their home country. A panel would need to examine, pursuant to footnote 10 to Article XVII, whether the same adverse effects would have occurred if another measure achieving the same goal would have been adopted, i.e. whether the measure was necessary.

In short, in our interpretation, footnote 10 to Article XVII would allow a panel to introduce a necessity test in Art XVII analysis. In our view, this follows inevitably from the concept of "inherence", which requires a counterfactual analysis of whether the regulation at hand constitutes a necessary condition for the same adverse effects to occur, the foreign character remaining the same.[114]

---

[114] It should be noted that the Panel in *Canada—Automotive Industry* has for a first time applied footnote 10, in response to an argument by Canada that with respect to "maintenance and repair work executed in Canada on buildings, machinery and equipment used for production purposes", there can be no discrimination against services supplied through modes 1 and 2, as cross-border supply and consumption abroad of these services are not technically feasible: "We consider that, although the supply of some repair and maintenance services on machinery and equipment through modes 1 and 2 might not be technically feasible, as they require the physical presence of the supplier, all other services listed by the complainants as being affected by the CVA requirements, including some consulting and advisory services relating to repair and maintenance of machinery, can be

3. The Perceived Redundancy of the Legitimate Policy Exception and Shift in Burden of Proof

Our proposal has to take other interpretative hurdles than the ordinary meaning of the National Treatment provisions in GATT and GATS. It can be argued that the most visible obstacles to the introduction of an integrated necessity test in this respect are the resulting redundancy of the legitimate policy exceptions lists and the shift in burden of proof: GATT Article XX and GATS Article XIV would become void of meaning, and the burden of proof as regards necessity would shift from defendant to complainant, who would have to demonstrate that a measure with adverse effects is unnecessarily trade-restrictive. These are then the same objections as some of those raised by the *Japan—Alcohol* panel against aims-and-effect, which indeed drew their authority from the Vienna Convention. In addition, it would be submitted that the lists of the policy exceptions are exhaustive in GATT and GATS, and that, although these lists are widely perceived as being far too limited,[115] it is hard to reconcile an unlimited expansion of this list with a Vienna Convention-conform interpretation. Conversely, another possible objection could be that, *de facto*, the variety of "connectors" found in GATT Article XX, all setting less stringent a standard than necessity, would be reduced to one single, more stringent standard.

We believe that none of these arguments is waterproof. As acknowledged by the Appellate Body, the WTO agreements, as international instruments, have to be interpreted and applied within the framework of the entire legal system prevailing at the time of interpretation.[116] It is not tenable to say

msupplied through modes 1 and 2. We further consider that treatment less favourable granted to services supplied outside Canada cannot be justified on the basis of inherent disadvantages due to their foreign character. Footnote 10 to Art. XVII only exempts Members from having to compensate for disadvantages due to foreign character in the application of the national treatment provision; it does not provide cover for actions which might modify the conditions of competition against services and service suppliers which are already disadvantaged due to their foreign character. We therefore find that lack of technical feasibility only excludes the supply of some repair and maintenance services on machinery and equipment through modes 1 and 2 from Canada's national treatment obligation. We also find that any eventual inherent disadvantages due to the foreign character of services supplied through modes 1 and 2 do not exempt Canada from its national treatment obligation with respect to the CVA requirements." Panel report on *Canada—Measures affecting the Automotive Industry, supra*, paras. 10.300–10–301.

[115] See Robert Hudec, *supra* n. 4, at 638; Aaditya Mattoo and Arvind Subramanian, "Regulatory Autonomy and Multilateral Disciplines: The Dilemma and a Possible Resolution," 1 *Journal of International Economic Law* (1998) 304, at 307; Frieder Roessler, "The Concept of Nullification and Impairment in the Legal System of the World Trade Organisation", in Ernst-Ulrich Peteromann (ed.) *International Trade Law and the GATT/WTO Dispute Settlement System* (1997), at 122.

[116] Appellate Body report on *United States—Import Prohibition of Certain Shrimp and Shrimp Products, supra* n. 37, para. 20, footnote 34, referring to *Namibia (Legal Consequences) Advisory Opinion* (1971) ICJ Rep, p. 31.

that the agenda of the modern Regulatory State is confined to the objectives enumerated in "an old, and often badly drafted, instrument."[117] This was explicitly confirmed by the panel in *Chile—Taxes* when it examined, in the context of GATT Article III, the necessity of the measures at hand, while declining to examine the legitimacy of the purported policy goals as such.[118] As evidenced by *Cassis de Dijon* in the EC context, once a measure is considered discriminatory because it causes adverse effects unnecessary to achieve the regulatory objective, exhaustive lists do not work any longer. Neither can it be said that an integrated necessity test would impinge more on regulatory autonomy then the current approach: as indicated earlier, the difference between the former and the latter is that one also imposes necessity, but only in regard to a limited number of permitted objectives, whereas the other would impose necessity with regard to any legitimate policy objective. It is entirely inconsistent to argue that one can not demand "efficiency" from Members' regulation, when the current WTO framework already requires such "efficiency," but only allows a limited number of objectives where that test needs to be fulfilled!

Also, the alleged shift in burden of proof should not be exaggerated: in accordance with a series of Appellate Body A rulings,[119] and as amply evidenced by panel and Appellate Body practice in relation to SPS cases,[120] a Member complaining that a measure is not unnecessarily trade-restrictive, will only be required to establish a *prima facie* case of inconsistency, i.e. raise a presumption that what claimed is true. When such a *prima facie* case is made, the burden of proof is shifted to the defending party, which must in turn refute the claimed inconsistency.[121] Since the Appellate Body has never provided any guidance as to the quantum of evidence required to meet the *prima facie* standard,[122] however, some commentators have posited that the presumption rule could easily be used as "a tool to support result-oriented findings," allowing adjudicators

---

[117] Robert Hudec, *supra* n. 4, at 633.

[118] Panel Report on *Chile—Taxes on Alcoholic Beverages, supra* n. 3, para. 7.148.

[119] See, most prominently, Appellate Body reports on *United States—Measures Affecting Imports of Woven Wool Shirts and Blouses* (WT/DS33/AB/R, adopted 23 May 1997), *EC— Measures concerning Meat and Meat Products (Hormones)* (WT/DS26/AB/R, adopted 13 February 1998).

[120] See *Japan—Measures Affecting Agricultural Products* (WT/DS76/AB/R, adopted 19 March 1999), *EC—Measures concerning Meat and Meat Products (Hormones) supra* n. 119, *Australia—Measures affecting Imports of Salmon* (WT/DS18/AB/R, adopted 6 November 1998).

[121] For a critique of the presumption rule, see Joost Pauwelyn, "Evidence, Proof and Persuasion in WTO Dispute Settlement: Who Bears the Burden?", 1 *Journal of International Economic Law* (1998) 227.

[122] Edwin Vermulst, Petros Mavroidis, Paul Waer, "The Functioning of the Appellate Body after Four Years: Towards Rule Integrity", 33 *Journal of World Trade* (1999) 1, 12; David Palmeter and Petros Mavroidis, *Dispute Settlement in the World Trade Organisation* (1999) 80.

"to decide that the burden of proof rests on, or has shifted to, that party which according to the panel and/or Appellate Body should lose."[123]

Moreover, in the recent *EC—Asbestos* panel Report, the panel seems to have abandoned this particular objection against the consideration of regulatory objectives under Article III:

> The burden of proof would not of course be greatly modified [by introducing a criterion on the risk of a product into the analysis of likeness within the meaning of Article III] because the EC would still have to prove the risk of the product, applying the principle of *probatio incumbit ejus que dixit.*[124]

And finally, as regards the textual redundancy of the policy exception provisions, one author has opined that inserting a necessity-like test into the National Treatment obligation would "take the sting off the criticism [. . .] of rendering Article XX redundant" because such an approach would "at least in spirit, [. . .] preserve all the useful safeguards in Article XX."[125] Alternatively, it has been suggested to subject *de facto* discriminatory measures to an integrated necessity test and never move to Article XX analysis for these measures, and continue to scrutinise *de jure* discriminatory measures under Article XX:

> Article XX only applies when there is a *facial* violation of the GATT obligations, as when a measure is origin-specific. Although Article XX does not refer to origin-specific measures, limiting Article XX to such violations can be inferred from the fact that Article III:2 can only apply to origin-neutral measures. The Article III:2 inquiry into whether products are "like" or "directly competitive" is only relevant if a panel is unsure if the measure is "applied . . . so as to afford protection to domestic production."[126]

Most recently, the Appellate Body in *EC—Asbestos* appears to have made a spectacular U-turn from the *Japan—Alcoholic Beverages* case law on the matter, and has ruled along the lines suggested above. After having ruled that the burden of proof would not be greatly modified by introducing a criterion on the risk of a product into the analysis of likeness, the panel had held:

> We nevertheless consider that other aspects that form part of the rights and obligations negotiated by the Members would be affected. Introducing the protection of human health and life into the likeness criteria would allow the

---

[123] Joost Pauwelyn, "Evidence, Proof and Persuasion in WTO Dispute Settlement: Who Bears the Burden?", 1 *Journal of International Economic Law* (1998) 227.

[124] Panel report on *European Communities—Measures Affecting Asbestos and Asbestos-Containing Products, supra* n. 43, para. 8.130. Emphasis added.

[125] Aaditya Mattoo and Arvind Subramaniain, "Regulatory Autonomy and Multilateral Disciplines: The Dilemma and a Possible Resolution", 1 *Journal of International Economic Law* 303, 314 (1998).

[126] Serena Wille, "Recapturing a Lost Opportunity: Article III:2 GATT 1994. *Japan—Taxes on Alcoholic Beverages* 1996", retrievable at the European Journal of International Law Website, www.ejil.org.

Member concerned to avoid the obligations in Article XX, particularly the test of necessity for the measure under paragraph (b) and the control exerted by the introductory clause to Article XX concerning any abuse of Article XX(b) when applying the measure.[127]

The Appellate Body, however, reversed this finding, stating that,

The fact that an interpretation of Article III:4, under those rules, implies a less frequent recourse to Article XX(b) does not deprive the exception in Article XX(b) of *effet utile*. Article XX(b) would only be deprived of *effet utile* if that provision could not serve to allow a Member to "adopt and enforce" measures "necessary to protect human . . . life or health".[128]

4. Contextual and Systemic Arguments: National Treatment, Standards Disciplines and Non-Violation

The GATT and GATS National Treatment provisions do not stand alone. They have to be read in context, notably the disciplines on domestic standards and the rules regarding non-violation complaints. An interpretation of National Treatment which imposes a necessity test on domestic regulation must be susceptible of a rational relationship to these rules.

(a) The Proposed Interpretation is Consistent with GATS Articles VI:5 and XXIII:3

GATS Article VI:5 represents a novel mingling of violation and non-violation concepts. It provides that in sectors in which a Member has undertaken specific commitments, pending the entry into force of disciplines developed in these sectors pursuant to Article VI:4, that Member shall not apply licensing and qualification requirements and technical standards that nullify or impair such specific commitments in a manner which does not comply with the criteria outlined in paragraph 4 and could not reasonably have been expected of that Member at the time the specific commitments in those sectors were made. In determining whether a Member is in conformity with the obligation under this provision, account shall be taken of international standards of relevant international organisations applied by that Member. By reference to paragraph 4 of the same provision, licensing and qualification requirements and technical standards ("LQTs") should be: (1) based on objective and transparent criteria, such as competence and the ability to supply the service; (2) not more burdensome than necessary to ensure

---

[127] Panel report on *European Communities—Measures Affecting Asbestos and Asbestos-Containing Products, supra* n. 43, para. 8.130. Emphasis added.
[128] Appellate Body report on *European Communities—Measures Affecting Asbestos and Asbestos-Containing Products, supra* n. 12, para. 115.

the quality of the service; and (3) in the case of licensing procedures, not in themselves a restriction on the supply of the service. If an LQT is not based on objective criteria, too burdensome or a restriction in itself, and could not have reasonably been expected, a violation complaint can now be launched against it on the basis of Article VI:5. But how would such a complaint relate to Articles XVII and XXIII:3? As a matter of clarity, several hypotheticals need to be distinguished.

1. The LQT is Based on Objective Criteria, but is Unnecessarily
   Restrictive

If an LQT is based on objective criteria, but is considered to be too burdensome, how would a complaint challenging such a LQT on the basis of Article VI:5 relate to Article XXIII:3?

First, what would happen if we apply the "traditional" interpretation of National Treatment (i.e. excluding a necessity test)? We observe that in the absence of the provision of Article VI:5, such a LQT could then only have been challenged on the basis of Article XXIII:3, *a priori* not on the basis of Article XVII. As a "genuine" non-violation complaint, it would clearly have been subject to more burdensome requirements. First, the complainant would have to provide a "detailed justification," and, second, she would have to show that the LQT has made a more than *de minimis* contribution to nullification and impairment. As indicated above, these requirements are absent from the violation track. In that respect, Article VI:5 would have somewhat mitigated the difficulty of challenging origin neutral regulatory barriers to services trade. On the other hand, the reasonable expectation requirement would in fact have "grandfathered" all such existing barriers resulting from LQTs, since it will be quasi-impossible for a complainant to demonstrate that it could not have been aware from a restriction which had already been in place at the time the commitments were scheduled.[129]

Second, if we would read a necessity test in Article XVII, could such an unnecessarily restrictive LQT already have been found discriminatory under Article XVII? An affirmative answer would provide a strong argument of redundancy against our proposed integrated necessity test: there would be no or very little use in having Article VI:5 alongside Article XVII. As we will demonstrate below, however, there is a strong argument in favour of answering this question in the negative.

2. The LQT is not Based on Objective Criteria

If the LQT at hand is not based on objective and transparent criteria—or, applying our proposal, has been found unnecessarily restrictive—and could not reasonably have been expected, it must be examined whether

---

[129] Patrick Low and Aaditya Mattoo, *supra* n. 22, at 9.

it would in any event have constituted a measure in breach of Article XVII's National Treatment obligation.

In the case of such LQTs affecting foreign service suppliers, let us first assume that the host state[130] had scheduled: (1) no quantitative restrictions on entry by foreign suppliers, (2) a general licensing requirement to verify reliability, and (3) a full National Treatment commitment. In such a case, it is not immediately clear whether a discriminatory/unnecessarily restrictive licensing practice would amount to a violation of National Treatment, since the scope of Article XVII has not been clearly defined. As explained by Mattoo, there are good arguments supporting both the thesis that Article XVII covers all measures affecting services supply, including measures affecting the right to establish ("pre-establishment measures"), and the thesis that Article XVII is only concerned with measures affecting the supply of services, once the supplier is established ("post-establishment measures").[131] Although that author argues that the rules of treaty interpretation mandate rather the first option, we submit that these interpretation rules may precisely warrant the opposite outcome. If discriminatory licensing in the above factual setting were to be covered by both Articles VI:5 and XVII, what would be the use of Article VI:5? After all, the reasonable expectation requirement imposes a very stringent discipline on those who wish to use that provision to challenge discriminatory licensing. This requirement, however, could be easily circumvented if Article XVII offered relief for one and the same problem. We argue, therefore, that the division of labour between Articles XVII and VI:5 is operated on *temporal* basis, not a *functional* one: Article XVII prohibits non-objective and unnecessary measures during post-establishment, Article VI:5 prohibits LQTs with those characteristics during pre-establishment. As a result, both provisions are complementary. This interpretation also supports our view that an integrated necessity test under Article XVII can perfectly coexist concurrently with Article VI:5. If Article XVII, including a necessity test, only applies to the post-establishment phase, there is no redundancy in having Article VI:5 regulating LQTs in the pre-establishment phase on the basis of objectiveness and least-restrictive means.

If we apply this theory to the hypothesis where, contrary to our first example, the host state has not scheduled a full National Treatment

---

[130] Licensing requirements, by their very nature, will only affect mode 3 services supply: only service suppliers who wish to establish a commercial presence in the host country may be required to apply for a licence. Qualification requirements and technical standards, on the contrary, will also affect the other supply modes. A license will normally be delivered only subsequent to prior verification of fulfilment of these requirements. Note, however, that the *Disciplines on Domestic Regulation in the Accountancy Sector* define, in para. 8, licensing requirements as "the substantive requirements, other than qualification requirements, to be satisfied in order to obtain or renew an authorisation to practice."

[131] Aaditya Mattoo, *supra* n. 18, at 114–15.

commitment, would it still be under a non-discrimination or necessity obligation as regards licensing pursuant to Article VI:5? It is worth recalling that the obligations of that provision only apply to "sectors in which Members have undertaken specific commitments." Consequently, if this phrase must be read as requiring commitments in both Market Access and National Treatment columns, the absence of a National treatment commitment would prevent a Member from relying on Article VI:5 to challenge discriminatory licensing. Such an interpretation would imply that a Member can not discriminate as regards licensing by virtue of Article VI:5 only if it has pledged not to discriminate, in the post-establishment phase, by virtue of commitments scheduled under Article XVII. On the contrary, if one accepts that "commitments" can be read, in connection with "sectors," as requiring only a Market Access commitment, the absence of a National Treatment commitment would not detract from the possibility to rely on Article VI:5. Of course, if a Member has not bound itself under Article XVII, it will be difficult to convince a panel that the complainant could not have reasonably expected "at the time the specific commitments in those sectors were made" that the host state would discriminate.

This type of interpretative problems are not merely hypothetical. When the Disciplines on Domestic Regulation in the Accountancy Sector were recommended for adoption to the Council for Trade in Services, the Chairman of the Working party on Professional Services added an informal Note, "Discussion of Matters relating to Articles XVI and XVII of the GATS in connection with the Disciplines on Domestic Regulation in the Accountancy Sector."[132] It was observed in this Note that "it became clear that some of these measures were subject to other legal provisions in the GATS, most notably Articles XVI and XVII," and that "the new disciplines developed under Article VI:4 must not overlap with [. . .] Articles XVI and XVII, as this would create legal uncertainty."[133] And while it was argued that "the disciplines to be developed under Article VI:4 cover domestic regulatory measures which [. . .] do not in principle discriminate against foreign suppliers," it was "also recognised that for some categories of measures the determination as to whether an individual measure falls under Article VI:4 disciplines or is subject to scheduling under Article XVII will require careful examination."[134]

(b) TBT and SPS

At first sight, the very existence of the TBT and SPS would also suggest there is a systemic argument against reading an integrated necessity test

---

[132] Document S/WPPS/4, at 9.
[133] *Ibid.*, para. 2.
[134] *Ibid.*, para. 3.

in GATT and GATS National Treatment. If Article III already allowed to arbitrate between legal and illegal origin-neutral measures using a necessity test, why then the need for these instruments in the first place, and why the dichotomy between TBT Articles 2.1 (National Treatment) and 2.2 (least restrictive means)? Alan Sykes, for one, has observed in this respect that the introduction of TBT Article 2.2[135] "went beyond the original GATT [. . .] because [it] extended the least restrictive means concept to measures that were consistent with the National Treatment obligation."[136] Having regard to the commands of Article 31 of the Vienna Convention, it seems then very difficult to frame TBT Article 2.1/SPS Article 2.3[137] as implying a necessity test, while this is exactly what TBT Article 2.2/SPS Article 5.6 provides, without voiding the latter of all meaning.

Again, we believe these arguments can be refuted. The first question— why these instruments if we have a necessity test in Article III?—is an easy one. As described in the second chapter of this book, these agreements do much more than explicitly imposing a necessity test as regards the measures covered by them. They impose new and substantive disciplines which are specific to the sectors they regulate.[138] The second one—how to explain the concurrent existence of "non-discrimination" and "necessity" provisions"—requires some elaboration. It can be argued that the non-discrimination provisions in TBT and SPS can be explained as addressing only *de jure* or facially discriminatory, origin-specific standards, whereas the necessity provisions cover *de facto* discriminatory, facially origin-neutral, measures. This makes sense, since these agreements do not contain a general exception provision which would allow justification of such *de jure* discrimination on the basis of environmental, health or safety reasons: there can simply be no plausible justification for origin-specific standards. This category should be a very narrow one. Standards which objectively differentiate can, however, as a collateral effect, adversely affect a particular group of producers, such as certain importers. These standards should be allowed only when they are necessary to achieve the legitimate policy goal.

---

[135] Art. 2.1 of the old Standards Code.
[136] Alan Sykes, *Product Standards for Internationally Integrated Goods Markets* (1995) 70.
[137] The SPS Agreement contains an additional non-discrimination obligation in Art. 5.5. Pursuant to Art. 5.5, each Member shall avoid arbitrary or unjustifiable distinctions in the levels it considers to be appropriate in different situations, if such distinctions result in discrimination or a disguised restriction on international trade. On this, see Joost Pauwelyn, "The WTO Agreement on SPS Measures as Applied in the First Three SPS Disputes", 2 *Journal of International Economic Law* (1999) 641, 653.
[138] See panel report on *EC—Measures concerning Meat and Meat Products (Hormones)*, *supra*, para. 8.38: "Many provisions of the SPS Agreement impose 'substantive' obligations which go significantly beyond and are additional to the requirements for invocation of Art. XX(b)." The panel quoted the provision on standardisation as an example.

Howse and Tuerk have advocated an alternative approach. They argue that many of the obligations in the TBT Agreement are of a "due process" character, ensuring transparency and integrity in the regulatory *process*. These authors posit that many features of the TBT Agreement would appear incomprehensible, but for an appreciation of its overall focus on regulatory processes. The example they use is precisely the National Treatment obligation contained in the TBT Agreement. According to the authors, this provision would be superfluous and inexplicable in the TBT Agreement, if that agreement were focused on the substance of regulations themselves, since Article III:4 of GATT already provides for a similar obligation.[139] This theory offers an equally plausible explanation for the concurrent existence of National Treatment and necessity provisions in the TBT Agreement: the National Treatment obligation would be of a purely procedural nature, whereas the necessity provision would continue to regulate the substance of the technical regulations.

5. A New Division of Labour with Non-Violation

An integrated necessity test would operate a novel distinction between violation and non-violation complaints: the only measures which could exclusively be challenged through a non-violation complaint, would, by definition, have to be "necessary measures." This would imply that a measure could be challenged because its juxtaposition with a foreign counterpart makes market access for foreign products/services harder. Although it may seem unlikely that a panel would strike down such a perfectly necessary domestic regulation in response to a non-violation complaint, there is no *a priori* reason why a measure which passed the Article XX test could not be challenged through a non-violation procedure. Indeed, nothing in the dispute settlement provisions of GATT or GATS and the DSU provides against that possibility. The marginalisation of the non-violation track which is likely to ensue, would be, in our view, a beneficial side-effect of this new division of labour.[140]

In this respect, it should be noted that the recent panel in *EC—Asbestos* has (1) explicitly confirmed the possibility that measures which have passed the Article XX test are the subject of a non-violation complaint,[141]

---

[139] Robert Howse and Elisabeth Tuerk, *supra* n. 11, at 308.

[140] *Cf.* Sung-Joon Cho, *supra* n. 42: "many future complaints that may be raised under the non-violation provision should be interpreted as violation cases if a Panel fully exercises its interpretative capacity in the context of the general obligations embodied in the GATT."

[141] Panel report on *European Communities—Measures Affecting Asbestos and Asbestos-Containing Products, supra* n. 12, para. 8.264: ". . . Art. XXIII:1(b) applies to a measure whether it is consistent with the GATT because the GATT does not apply to it or is justified by Art. XX." Confirmed by the Appellate Body (see *supra*).

but, at the same time, (2) has introduced a "stricter burden of proof" in relation to such measures.[142]

D. GOOD FAITH PERFORMANCE OF NATIONAL TREATMENT OBLIGATIONS AS A PROXY FOR OPTIMAL CARE IN INTERNATIONAL TRADE

We have explained above how our proposal would remedy the flaws of the current case law, and how the Vienna Convention can be understood to support our proposal. In this subsection, we will suggest a complementary and final argument in support of our thesis. We submit that:

—WTO Members which are bound by a National Treatment obligation, must, pursuant to their good faith obligations under Public International Law (PIL), avoid to cause imports-specific adverse effects;
—this good faith performance of a National Treatment obligation functions as a proxy for the choice by WTO Members of an optimal level of care in international trade.

In the very first report it issued, the then newly established Appellate Body solemnly stated that WTO law should not be read "in clinical isolation" from PIL.[143] In addition, it considers Articles 31 and 32 of the Vienna Convention a codification of customary rules of PIL, which it is directed to apply by Article 3:2 DSU when interpreting the WTO agreements.[144] Article 31:1 provides, *inter alia*, that a treaty shall be interpreted in good faith. These rulings make clear that the obligation of good faith performance and interpretation of treaty obligations,[145] as embedded in Articles 26 and 31 of the Vienna Convention, respectively, is part and parcel of WTO law.[146]

We argue that an integrated necessity test is simply an articulation of this PIL concept of good faith performance and interpretation of treaty obligations. The adverse effects of domestic regulation can be randomly distributed among domestic and imported products/services. As we have stated time and again, not all instances where imported products/services suffer adverse effects from regulation should give rise to a breach of National Treatment. We have argued above that the ordinary

---

[142] *Ibid.*, para. 8.281–282. Not addressed upon appeal.
[143] Appellate Body report on *United States—Standards for Reformulated and Conventional Gasoline, supra* n. 36, p. 17.
[144] See footnote 13 of ch. 1, and references there.
[145] See, generally, Elisabeth Zoller, *La Bonne Foi en Droit International Public* (1977); JF O'Connor, *Good Faith in International Law* (1991).
[146] See David Palmeter and Petros Mavroidis, *supra* n. 122, at 53.

meaning of "not according no less favourable treatment" is the causation of adverse effects specific to imported products/services. The scope of this obligation, however, needs to be interpreted in good faith. This implies, in our view, that the regulating Member should be required to make a *bona fide* effort to avoid the causation of such adverse effects. Avoidable effects are those effects which are unnecessary to reach the regulatory objective. A Member which acts in good faith under WTO law will not apply unnecessarily restrictive regulation.

As a matter of fact, the Appellate Body has stated that GATT Article XX's chapeau—a prohibition of arbitrary or unjustifiable discrimination in the pursuance of legitimate policy objectives—is "merely an expression of the principle of good faith in international law."[147] We have demonstrated above that panels have based their "arbitrary or unjustifiable discrimination" findings under the chapeau of GATT Article XX on the same grounds as their finding of a lack of "necessity" under GATT Article XX(b). We have inferred from that that there is no difference in substance between arbitrarily or unjustifiably discriminatory regulation and unnecessary regulation, arguing that regulation is unjustifiable or arbitrary when it is avoidable and unnecessary.[148] The logical conclusion to all this would be that necessity, in the words of the Appellate Body, is also merely an expression of the principle of good faith in PIL.

This reading of National Treatment in the light of good faith discipline does little more than requiring WTO Members to choose their optimal level of care in their regulatory activity. Indeed, the choice between an interpretation of the National Treatment obligation which either:

—mandates an integrated necessity test,
—does not require such a test and leaves Members free to adopt unnecessary regulation, or
—holds Members responsible for any and all adverse effects resulting from their regulation, whether the latter can be considered necessary or not,

can be usefully analogised to the choice of the level of optimal care in torts. Indeed, an integrated necessity test could be regarded as doing nothing but requiring the regulating Member to choose its optimal level of care under a negligence rule.

The most common economic definition of negligence can be seen in operation in Judge Learned Hand's famous opinion, *US* v. *Carroll Towing Co.* (159 F.2d 169, 174 (2nd Circuit 1947)). The events that gave rise to the case were as follows. Several barges owned by the

---

[147] Apellate Body report on *United States—Import Prohibition of Certain Shrimp and Shrimp Products*, *supra* n. 37, para. 48.

[148] See *supra*, p. 64 under heading 'The Relationship National Treatment—Legitimate Policy Exceptions.'

Connors Marine Co. were tied together off a busy Manhattan Pier. The defendant's tug boat, "Carroll," removed one of the lines connecting the barges to the pier. When the remaining lines broke, the barges were washed down-river and sank. No one was aboard the barges when they broke away, and the evidence indicated that had Connors' barge operator (the "bargee") been on board, the barges could have been saved. The question for the Court was whether Connors was liable for failing to have its "bargee" remain aboard. Judge Learned Hand wrote that Connor's liability for the lost barge depended on: (1) The probability that she will break away; (2) the gravity of the resulting injury, if she does; (3) the burden of adequate precautions. In algebraic terms: if the probability be called **P**; the injury, **L**; and the burden, **B**; liability depends upon whether **B** is less than **L** multiplied by **P**: i.e., whether **B** less than **PL**. A defendant is negligent if and only if **B** < **PL**. This formulation of the negligence rule has come to be known as the Hand Formula. Judge Learned Hand went on to conclude that, taking into account the surrounding circumstances (there were strong winds, the harbor was busy, and the ship's cargo valuable), the risk (**PL**) outweighed the burden of prevention (**B**). Consequently, he held Connors liable.

Graphically, the Hand formula can be represented as follows:

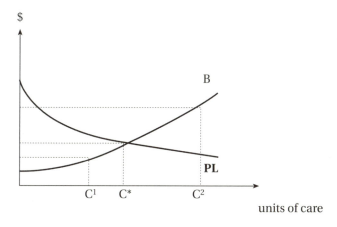

Graph 1. The Hand Curve

The X-axis depicts the amount of care taken by the defendant. The Y-axis represents the cost of taking precautions (line **B**) or of the expected loss resulting from failing to take precautions (line **PL**). The upward slope of line **B** indicates that the marginal cost of prevention increases as more care is taken. The downward slope of line **PL** indicates that the marginal expected cost of an accident declines as more care is taken. The point at which the combined cost of precautions and accident are minimised is the optimal level of care, represented by C^*.

When we apply the *Hand formula* towards a proper interpretation of the National Treatment obligation, it can be readily observed that the current case law sets the standard of care as regards the regulating importing Member either too low (*Gas Guzzler*[149]), say at C^1, or too high (*Japan— Alcoholic Beverages* cases), say at C^2. It is clear that in the *Gas Guzzler* case, for instance, the tremendous loss for the exporting Members resulting from the regulations could have been avoided at a cost B which was inferior to PL, especially given the high probability factor P (the adverse effects of the regulation on exporting Members were perfectly foreseeable). The *Japan—Alcoholic Beverages* case law, on the other hand, arguably introduces a construction which stops short of introducing strict liability, but for some covert and discretionary judicial moderation of a clear-cut effects-based discrimination test. It is virtually impossible to avoid that the random distribution of regulation's adverse effects falls sometimes heavier on exporting Members, but for a prohibitively high cost to avoid such effects. B is clearly greater than PL for such adverse effects.

In fact, the levels of care chosen by the regulating Member under the *Gas Guzzler* and *Japan—Alcoholic Beverages* case law represent the optimal level of care for the regulating Member under, respectively, a no and strict liability rule. When we represent these three options in a game theoretical framework, the superiority of the necessity test over either strict or no liability rules becomes apparent:

Given that:	Assuming that:
IM = importing Member (regulator)	**L** = 200 if both take care (reflecting
EM = exporting Member	the reality that foreign regulation in
C = care (necessary regulation by	itself causes an unavoidable
IM,adaptation efforts by EM)	adverse effect on exporters)
NC = no care (unnecessary	**L** = 600 if either one takes care
regulation by IM,	**L** = 1000 if none takes care
no adaptation efforts by EM)	**B** for IM = 100

---

[149] In *United States—Taxes on Automobiles*, (DS31/R, unadopted), at issue was, among other things, a US tax on low fuel economy automobiles. A vast majority of the automobiles subject to the tax happened to be imported. The Panel ruled that the tax was not discriminatory because (1) there was, in its view, no protectionist intent, and (2) the technology to produce high fuel economy cars was not "inherently" confined to US producers. Put another way, foreign producers could, *potentially*, adapt their production and align it to US production, and, doing so, avoid the tax. Thus, according to this ruling, as long as foreign producers have the *capability* to adapt their production to the characteristics of domestic production, regardless of the cost such adaptation may imply, there is no violation of the National Treatment obligation.

L = loss
B = burden of taking optimal care

B for EM = 1000 (reflecting the prohibitive cost for exporters to adapt their products and services to every unnecessary regulation in each target jurisdiction)

Negligence Rule (cf. integrated necessity test à la *Chile—Alcoholic Beverages*)

		IM	
		C	NC
EM	C	−100,−1200	−600, −1000
	NC	−100, −600	−1000, 0

Both IM and EM have a dominant strategy: IM will care, EM will not. The resulting Nash equilibrium is Pareto-efficient. The cost of regulatory heterogeneity is distributed between IM and EM, with EM clearly carrying the largest part of the burden.

No liability (cf. *Gas Guzzler* case law)

		IM	
		C	NC
EM	C	−100,−1200	0, −1600
	NC	−100, −600	0, −1000

Both IM and EM have again a dominant strategy: neither of them will care. The resulting Nash equilibrium (NC-NC) is Kaldor-Hicks-inferior (the C-NC pay-off is Kaldor-Hicks superior). The entire cost of unnecessary regulation by IM is passed on to EM, something which the Appellate Body in *Korea—Beef* considered to be a pertinent "indicator" of an unnecessary burdensome regulation.[150] Note that the Gas Guzzler outcome is here represented by the pay-off NC-C, which is even Pareto-inferior to the NC-NC pay-off. See table over.

Both IM and EM have again a dominant strategy, resulting in the C-NC Nash equilibrium. Although this equilibrium is Pareto-optimal, and Kalder-Hicks equivalent to the C-NC pay-off under a necessity rule, there are, in our view, two, non-economic, considerations which should prevail:

---

[150] Appellate Body report on *Korea—Measures Affecting Imports of Fresh, Chilled and Frozen Beef, supra* n. 109, para. 181.

Strict Liability (cf. *Japan—Alcoholic Beverages* case law)

		IM	
		C	NC
EM	C	−300,−1000	−600, −1000
	NC	−700, −0	−1000, 0

—first, there is a clear redistribution effect, in that a regulating Member would have to carry the cost of all its regulation's adverse effects on all exporting Members;

—second, any strict liability regime tends to encourage activity level changes by the defendant.[151] In our case, this would imply that IM would, as a result, adopt *less* regulation, rather than restricting itself to *necessary* regulation.

Both consequences would be translated in a chilling effect on regulatory activity *in general*, which was clearly never intended by the drafters of the WTO agreements. We therefore take the view that an integrated necessity test is preferable to an effects-based test. It constitutes the optimal level of care which WTO Members are bound to choose in the light of their obligation to perform the treaty obligation of National Treatment in good faith.

E. CAVEAT: MAKING NECESSITY "ADJUDICATABLE"

From the preceding sections, we conclude that there are strong policy and legal grounds for equating non-discrimination with the requirement of a necessity test as regards origin-neutral measures. But this conclusion in turn begs two interrelated questions. First, are WTO adjudicators actually *capable* of adjudicating the question whether a measure is not more than necessary to achieve a domestic policy goal? Efficient regulation is a notoriously difficult exercise, independently from what international agreements may require. Regulators often fail to achieve their policy objectives, and equally often achieve those objectives in an inefficient manner. Can WTO adjudicators be expected to make sound—or, indeed, sound*er*—assessments as regards the necessity of domestic regulation which specifically and adversely affects foreign products or services? Second, even if WTO adjudicators are capable of assessing necessity, is there not a "legitimacy" or "balance of powers" argument

---

[151] See, for instance, Steven Shavell, "Strict Liability versus Negligence", 9 *Journal of Legal Studies* (1980) 1, 2.

against panels scrutinising domestic regulation for unnecessary effects? The former question has to do with capacity, the latter with legitimacy. They are, however, closely related.

It should be recalled that the powers of WTO adjudicators are circumscribed by the proviso of Article 3.2 DSU. As was demonstrated in *Chile— Alcoholic Beverages*, however, this provision does not have many teeth: Chile argued before the Appellate Body that the necessity test arguably conducted by the panel in its Article III:2 analysis "added to the rights and obligations of Members," thereby acting inconsistently with Article 3.2 DSU. The Appellate Body, however, rejected the argument. According to the Appellate Body, when a panel interpretation is found to be correct, the panel report will not have added to or diminished the Members' rights and obligations: "we have difficulty in envisaging circumstances in which a panel could add to the rights and obligations of a Member of the WTO if its conclusions reflected a correct interpretation and application of provisions of the covered agreements."[152] Put another way, if the Appellate Body thinks that the panel's interpretation is fine, both judges have appropriately discharged their duties under the DSU. *Point final.* Consequently, since we are convinced that our proposal to interpret National Treatment as requiring a necessity test regarding origin-neutral measures is legally the appropriate one, we naturally submit that, in that respect, we see no problem in having WTO adjudicators conducting necessity tests 7/7 24/24.

However, this is just the easy answer (albeit an important one). In the trade academic circuit there is a lot of talk lately—partially fed by a climate of popular globalisation rebuke—about "legitimacy" and the "constitutionalisation" of the WTO. Europeans know all too well what (at least part of) this debate boils down to: the so-called democratic deficit caused by a shift in decision-making power from national parliaments to a faceless, non-directly elected, supranational bureaucracy in Brussels, resulting in calls for "subsidiarity" etc etc. Should our proposal provoke similar criticism and/or emotions as regards the WTO?

A distinction here should be made between criticism which can be considered *relative*, i.e. judging the merits of our proposal as compared to the status quo in WTO law, and criticism which is *absolute*, i.e. rejecting, *per se*, the idea of WTO adjudicators inquiring into the necessity of domestic regulation specifically and adversely affecting imported products or foreign services/service suppliers.

When one compares the outcome of our proposal with the status quo, we fail to see the case against the integrated necessity test on "legitimacy" grounds. GATT/WTO Panels have been conducting necessity

---

[152] Appellate Body report on *Chile—Taxes on Alcoholic Beverages*, (WT/DS87/AB/R, adopted 12 January 2000), para. 79.

tests regarding *de facto* discriminatory measures under Article XX for decades. Why should there be a big fuzz all of a sudden? Moreover, our proposal would avoid the—indeed unjustifiable—restriction by GATT Article XX/GATS Article XIV to a limited number of policy objectives. One would expect the pro-deference champions to be happy with that aspect of our proposal. Furthermore, we have demonstrated earlier that our proposal would actually enhance transparency and legitimacy, as compared to the status quo: adjudicators will now at least be obliged to give reasons for finding *de facto* discrimination, instead of covering up their seat-of-the-pants judgments with "fuzzy" language. An explicitly reasoned finding on necessity will be exposed to close public scrutiny.

A more solid argument can be raised, perhaps, relating to the capacity of WTO adjudicators *as such* to deal with necessity. This argument does not assess our proposal against the background of current WTO arrangements and interpretations, but questions the merits of the existing system as such, where adjudicators are already allowed to make necessity assessments. These critics would submit that WTO adjudicators should not be allowed to sit in the driver's seat as far as domestic regulatory choices are concerned, because they are not capable of making the right choices for the people.

Here again a distinction should be made. There are different meanings to "capacity", a narrow and a broader one, and the respective criticisms should be addressed accordingly. Within the narrow meaning of capacity, the question is: how can judges know *ex post* what policy instrument is necessary, and no more than that, or, alternatively, *ex ante*, what less restrictive instrument is available? We will refer to this as capacity *sensu strictu*. However, regulatory capacity also implies an accurate understanding of the specific characteristics and needs of the citizens subject to regulation, the "regulatees". This is the issue of having international adjudicators "second-guess" domestic regulatory choices. We will refer to this as capacity *sensu latu*.

As regards adjudicators' capacity *sensu strictu* to deal with regulatory necessity, we fail to see why they would not have the technical competence to make these necessity judgements, provided that they can seek information from any source and call upon technical experts when required.[153] It

---

[153] See, along the same lines, Don Regan, "The Dormant Commerce Clause and 'Dumb Duck Disease' ", paper presented at the World Trade Forum 2000 conference "The Role of the Judge: Lessons for the WTO" (on file with the author), at 67. After having made his case against judicial "value balancing" (full proportionality in EC parlance) on legitimacy grounds, he writes:

> [. . .] it is worth noting that there is one kind of case where the court might engage in a sort of degenerate "balancing" without being required to make any value judgement at all. That is the case where the court finds as an empirical matter that the law under review does not achieve any of the putative benefit. If there really is no benefit, then no normative judgement comparing values is required. Even here, we might think the court should not second-guess the legislature on the empirical judgement. [. . .] *But in truth, there may be some empirical judgements that the court can make as well as the legis*

should be recalled in that respect that WTO panels have broad powers to seek information from any source and consult experts pursuant to Article 13 of the DSU. In the context of Article 5.6 of the SPS agreement, for instance, recourse has often been taken by SPS Panels to scientific experts to advise them as to what measure is necessary and what is not.[154]

However, even though WTO adjudicators may be technically capable of making necessity assessments, it could still be argued that domestic regulators are more familiar with the specific needs of their "regulatees," and have, therefore, a greater capacity *sensu latu*. This is basically the subsidiarity/legitimacy argument. A good example is consumer protection. Some States believe their consumers need more and heavier protection against deceiving practices than other. An assessment of what is necessary to protect consumers will consequently vary from one State to the other. As a result, if consumer protection regulation in a particular State is challenged in the course of international dispute settlement procedures, an international adjudicator will have to decide how vulnerable the consumers in a particular State are, and how to best protect their interests. However, even though she would not touch upon the goal of consumer protection as such, the international adjudicator will be lead to impose her vision of the "average" consumer in all Member States. The resulting "negative harmonisation" is a feature commonly attributed the ECJ case law on the EC Freedom provisions, where the ECJ has been led to base its findings on the basis of an abstract "reasonably circumspect consumer" assumption. As Stephen Weatherill has pointed out, in these cases

> [t]he European Court, in adjudicating on the validity of a trade-restrictive national measure, is engaged in a balance between the interests of the

lature [. . .]. [But] to say the court can do as well as the legislature is not to say they can better, and I see little reason to think they can. So, the case for judicial deference may be at its weakest here, but it still seems that, other things being equal, we might prefer that the decision be made by the politically responsive body. [. . .] (emphasis added)

It should be noted, though, that the WTO adjudicator will not always be able to make the necessity finding "as an emprical matter". See for instance the recent panel report on *Korea—Measures Affecting Imports of Fresh, Chilled and Frozen Beef, supra* n. 41, deciding a GATT Art. III:4 claim and an Art. XX(d) defence, which confirmed that a panel may be compelled to go beyond empirical findings when assessing the "necessity" of domestic regulation, and, rather, base its findings on "projections, based on those facts, regarding what [a WTO Member] reasonably could do" to achieve its purported policy objective in an efficient manner. In this case, the Panel effectively disagreed with the defendant that a concrete regulatory instrument would be such an effective instrument and suggested another one—the imposition of fines for breach—instead: "The effectiveness of fines will depend, on the one hand, on the level of such fines and the probability of being caught and, on the other hand, on the level of profit margin resulting from such fraud. The Panel considers that the threat of prosecution, which for small butchers would imply an attack on their reputation, would be an effective deterrent." *Ibid.*, para. 669.

[154] See, in particular, the panel report on *Australia—Measures affecting Imports of Salmon, supra* n. 120.

consumers who are thought (by national authorities) to need protection and the group of consumers which the Court reckons stand to benefit from deregulation.[155]

Transposed into the WTO context, this dilemma is of course exacerbated, since WTO Panels may be called upon to assess the necessity of consumer protection in States with far greater regulatory divergence as between them than within the relatively homogenous community of EU Member States. What is necessary to protect the consumer in, say, Malawi may differ quite a bit from what is necessary in the United States or the EC.

In the light of the above, it is clear that necessity cannot be a uniform and stringent standard. It requires a certain degree of flexibility in its implementation. We submit that WTO law, in particular in the light of the Appellate Body's recent interpretation of "necessary" in GATT Article XX, allows for such flexibility. The WTO necessity test requires Panels to take into account "reasonable availability" and "technical and economic feasibility" of alternative measures. It can, in our view, very well be argued that a stringent consumer protection law in one country, in the light of the perceived vulnerability of the local consumer, would be the only "reasonably available" measure, and hence WTO-consistent, whereas the same regulation may not be the only reasonable available measure in another country, where consumers are supposedly less vulnerable. There is no reason why one regulation could be necessary in one country, but unnecessary in another. A "reasonableness" qualifier leaves ample discretion to the adjudicator and allows deference to domestic choices in difficult and politically sensitive cases.[156]

As a matter of fact, as stated earlier, the Appellate Body's recent observations regarding necessity in *Korea—Beef* and *EC—Asbestos* have explicitly *equated*[157] this reasonable availability standard described by

---

[155] Stephen Weatherill, "Recent Case Law concerning the Free Movement of Goods: Mapping the Frontiers of Market Deregulation", 36 *Common Market Law Review* (1999) 51, at 55.

[156] The panel report on *European Communities—Measures Affecting Asbestos and Asbestos-Containing Products, supra* n. 43, recently also shed some light on what alternative measures a Member could be "reasonably" expected to employ. According to the panel, the fact that, administratively, one measure may be easier to implement than another does not mean that the other measure is not reasonably available. The existence of a reasonably available measure would need to be assessed in the light of the economic and administrative realities facing the Member concerned. Para. 8.207 of the panel report.

[157] Appellate Body report on *Korea—Measures Affecting Imports of Fresh, Chilled and Frozen Beef, supra* n. 109, para. 166: "The standard described by the panel in *United States—Section 337* encapsulates the general considerations we have adverted to above. In our view, the weighing and balancing process we have outlined is comprehended in the determination of whether a WTO-consistent alternative measure which the Member concerned could 'reasonably be expected to employ' is available, or whether a less WTO-inconsistent measure is 'reasonably available'."

the panel in *United States—Section 337* with a "weighing and balancing process" which seems to allow considerable flexibility to WTO adjudicators in their "necessity" determinations. Indeed, the Appellate Body stated that determination of whether a measure, which is not "indispensable", may nevertheless be "necessary" within the contemplation of Article XX(d), involves in every case a process of weighing and balancing a series of factors, including: (1) the contribution made by the compliance measure to the enforcement of the law or regulation at issue, (2) the importance of the common interests or values protected by that law or regulation, and (3) the accompanying impact of the law or regulation on imports or exports. Along those lines, the Appellate Body concluded that, the more vital or important the common interests or values are, the easier it would be to accept as "necessary" a measure designed as an enforcement instrument;[158] that, the greater the contribution, the more easily a measure might be considered to be "necessary";[159] and that a measure with a relatively slight impact upon imported products might more easily be considered as "necessary" than a measure with intense or broader restrictive effects.[160]

This dictum is quite extraordinary. Although the panels and the Appellate Body have traditionally stated that WTO law is not concerned with the choice of legitimate policy goals as such, but rather with the choice of the means to reach the policy goal, the Appellate Body here explicitly allows WTO adjudicators to assess the "importance" of the "common interest or values" at stake. Although it would surely be undesirable *per se* that a WTO adjudicator says which "common values" are more important than others, or, indeed, even tell an individual Member the membership what those "common values" are,[161] it is important to note that the balancing exercise proposed by the Appellate Body should only take place in the context of determining whether a measure is necessary to reach an objective, although it cannot be considered "indispensable." This implies that the balancing is only used to *soften* the

---

[158] *Ibid.*, para. 162.
[159] *Ibid.*, para. 163.
[160] *Ibid.*
[161] Along the same lines, Robert Howse and Elisabeth Tuerk, *supra* n. 11, at 326: "One appealing view of Art. XX is that it deals with the potential tension between trade liberalisation and other values, through a series of provisions that scrutinise the relation of means to ends, rather than the value of the ends pursued themselves, provided those ends fall within a discrete head of Art. XX. Does the AB really have the legitimacy to say to a society that, for instance, the pursuit of religious purity or piety is a less compelling objective than the protection of human health? Does it have the *bona fides* to make a determination that the rights of people count for more than the "rights" of animals? We would suggest that to remain consistent with its role a treaty interpreter under Art. 31 of the *Vienna Convention*, whenever the AB is hierarchising objectives within the heads of Art. XX, it must do so following the hierarchies implicit or explicit in international law more generally."

standard of indispensability in function of the policy objective at issue, and not to make it more stringent.[162] The purpose of the balancing exercise proposed by the Appellate Body is therefore clearly to allow more flexibility to WTO adjudicators in their necessity determinations, taking into account the policy objective pursued and the trade impact of the measure. This new case law should contribute to appeasing concerns that WTO adjudicators would adopt a rigid necessity test which fails to show deference to domestic needs and particularities.

---

[162] *Ibid.*, at 325: "In fact [the Appellate Body] is introducing balancing so as, to provide Members with an *additional* 'margin of appreciation' in making regulatory choices to achieve the purposes stated in those provisions of Art. XX, that entail a necessity test."

List of Cited Cases

C. EUROPEAN COURT OF JUSTICE DECISIONS

Selective Bibliography

Aly K. Abu-Akeel, "The MFN as it Applies to Services Trade: New Problems for an Old Concept", 33 *Journal of World Trade* (1999) 103

Alexandre Bernel, *Le Principe d' Equivalence ou de "Reconnaissance Mutuelle" en Droit Communautaire* (1996)

Hugues Calvet and Franck Dintilhac, "Chronique de Jurisprudence en matière de Liberté d'Etablissement et de Libre prestation de Services", 27 *Revue Trimestrielle de Droit Européen* (1991) 59

Sung-Joon Cho, "GATT Non-Violation Issues in the WTO Framework: Are they the Achilles' Heel of the Dispute Settlement Process?", 39 *Harvard International Law Review* (1998) 311

—— *Case Note*, retrievable at the European Journal of International Law website, www.ejil.org

Thomas Cottier and Kristina Nadakavukaren Schefer, "Non-Violation Complaints in WTO/GATT Dispute Settlement: Past, Present and Future", in Ernst-Ulrich Petersmann (ed.), *International Trade Law and the GATT/WTO Dispute Settlement System* (1997)

Paul Craig and Gráinne de Búrca, *EC Law: Text, Cases and Materials* (1995)

Bill Davey and Joost Pauwelyn, "MFN Unconditionality: A Legal Analysis of the Concept in View of its Evolution in the GATT/WTO Jurisprudence with Particular Reference to the Issue of 'Like Product' ", in Thomas Cottier and Petros Mavroidis (eds.) *Regulatory Barriers and the Principle of Non-Discrimination in World Trade Law* (2000) 36

Lucette Defalque, "Le Concept de Discrimination en Matière de Libre Circulation des Marchandises", *Cahiers de droit Europeen* (1987) 471

Sara Dillon, "Fuji-Kodak, the WTO, and the death of Domestic Political Constituencies", 8 *Minnesota Journal of Global Trade* (1999) 197

James Durling and Simon Lester, "Original Meanings and the Film Dispute: The Drafting History, Textual Evolution, and Application of the Non-Violation Nullification and Impairment Remedy", 32 *George Washington Journal of International Law* (1999) 211

Piet Eeckhout, "After Keck and Mithouard: Free Movement of Goods in the EC, Market Access, and Non-Discrimination", in Thomas Cottier, Petros Mavroidis and Patrick Blatter (eds.), *Regulatory Barriers and the Principle of Non-Discrimination in World Trade Law* (2000)

—— "The EC Response", paper presented at the World Trade Forum 2000 conference "The Role of the Judge: Lessons for the WTO"

Claus-Dieter Ehlermann and Gianluigi Campogrande, "Rules on Services in the EEC: A Model for Negotiating World-Wide Rules?" in Ernst Ulrich Petersmann and Meinhard Hilf (eds.) *The New GATT Round of Multilateral Trade Negotiations* (1990) 481

Lothar Ehring, "Non-Discrimination in WTO Law: National and Most-Favoured-Nation Treatment or Equal Treatment?", *Jean Monnet Seminar Paper*, Harvard University, 2001.

Energy Charter Treaty Secretariat, *The Energy Charter Treaty and Related Documents* (1995)

Daniel Farber and Robert Hudec, "Free Trade and the Regulatory State: A GATT's-Eye View of the Dormant Commerce Clause", 47 *Vanderbilt Law Review* 1401

Bimal Ghosh, *Gains from Global Linkages: Trade in Services and Movement of Persons* (1997)

Edward Graham, "Competition Policy and the New Trade Agenda", in Pierre Sauve and Americo B. Zampetti (eds.), *New Dimensions of Market Access in a Globalising World Economy* (1995) 105

H.L.A. Hart and A.M. Honoré, *Causation in the Law* (1959)

Vassilis Hatzopoulos, "Comments on Alpine Investments", *Common Market Law Review* (1995) 1436

Bernard Hoekman and Petros Mavroidis, "Competition, Competition Policy and the GATT", 17 *The World Economy* (1994) 121

—— and Pierre Sauve, *Liberalizing Trade in Services* 3 (World Bank Discussion Paper No 243) (1994)

Robert Howse and Don Regan, "The Product/Process distinction—An Illusory Basis for Disciplining Unilateralism in Trade Policy", 11 *European Journal of International Law* (2000) 249

Robert Howse and Elisabeth Tuerk, "The WTO Impact on Internal Regulations—A Case Study of the Canada—EC Asbestos Dispute", in Graínne De Búrca and Joanne Scott (eds.) *The EU and the WTO: Legal And Constitutional Aspects* (2001)

Robert Hudec, "GATT/WTO Constraints on Domestic Regulation: Requiem for an 'Aims and Effects' Test", 32 *The International Lawyer* (1998) 623

Jean Guy Huglo, "Chronique de Jurisprudence en matière de Liberté d'Etablissement et de Libre prestation de Services", 28 *Revue Trimestrielle de Droit Europeen* (1992) 687

—— "Chronique de Jurisprudence en matière de Liberté d'Etablissement et de Libre prestation de Services", 29 *Revue Trimestrielle de Droit Europeen* (1993) 655

—— "Chronique de Jurisprudence en matière de Liberté d'Etablissement et de Libre prestation de Services", 30 *Revue Trimestrielle de Droit Europeen* (1994) 465

—— "Chronique de Jurisprudence en matière de Liberté d'Etablissement et de Libre prestation de Services", 31 *Revue Trimestrielle de Droit Europeen* (1995) 827

—— "Chronique de Jurisprudence en matière de Liberté d'Etablissement et de Libre prestation de Services", 32 *Revue Trimestrielle de Droit Europeen* (1996) 741

John H. Jackson, *The World Trading System* (1997)

Miles Kahler, "Trade and Domestic Differences", in Suzanne Berger and Ronald Dore (eds.) *National Diversity and Global Capitalism* (1996)

Louis Kaplow, "Rules versus Standards: An Economic Analysis", 42 *Duke Law Journal* (1992) 557

P.J.G. Kapteyn and P. Verloren van Themaat, *Introduction to the Law of the European Communities* (1998)

Kazumochi Kometani, "Trade and Environment: How Should WTO Panels Review Environmental Regulations under GATT Articles III and XX", 16 *Northwestern Journal of International Law and Business* (1996) 441.

Norio Komuro, "Kodak-Fuji Film Dispute and the WTO Panel Ruling", 32 *Journal of World Trade* (1998) 161

Koen Lenaerts, "L'Egalité de Traitement en Droit Communautaire. Un Principe Unique aux Apparences Multiples", 27 *Cahiers de Droit Europeen* (1991) 3

Patrick Low and Aaditya Mattoo, "Is There a Better Way? Alternative Approaches to Liberalisation under the GATS", (1999) mimeo

John Mackie, "Causes and Conditions", 4 *American Philosophical Quarterly* 245 (1965); reprinted as Chapter I in Ernest Sosa and Michael Tooley (eds.) *Causation* (1993) 33

Mario Marconini, "The Uruguay Round Negotiations on Services: An Overview", in Patrick Messerlin and Karl Sauvant (eds.) *The Uruguay Round. Services in the World Economy* (1990) 19

Giuliano Marenco, "Pour une Interprétation Traditionelle de la Notion de Mesure d'Effet Equivalent à une Restriction Quantitative", *Cahiers de Droit Europeen* (1984) 291

—— "The Notion of Restriction on the Freedom of Establishment and Provision of Services in the Case Law of the Court", *Yearbook of European Law* (1992) 111

Aaditya Mattoo, "National Treatment in the GATS—Corner Stone or Pandora's Box?", 31 *Journal of World Trade* (1997) 107

—— "MFN and the GATS", in Thomas Cottier, Petros Mavroidis, Patrick Blatter (eds.) *Regulatory Barriers and the Principle of Non-Discrimination of World Trade Law: Past, Present and Future* (1999)

—— and Arvind Subramanaian, "Regulatory Autonomy and Multilateral Disciplines: The Dilemma and a Possible Resolution", 1 *Journal of International Economic Law* (1998) 303

Patrick Messerlin, "Regulatory Reforms in Services and Commercial Policy: The Case of Developing Countries", (1999) mimeo

Won Mog Choi, *Progressive Interpretation of The Concepts of "Like" And "Directly Competitive Or Substitutable" Products in the GATT/WTO Agreement: The Likeness-Substitutability Problem Of Goods*, unpublished S.J.D. Dissertation, Georgetown University Law Center, 2001

Kalypso Nicolaides and Joel Trachtman, "From Policed Regulation to Managed Recognition: Mapping the Boundary in GATS", paper presented at the "Services 2000: New Directions in Trade Liberalisation" conference, Washington DC, 1999

J.F. O'Connor, *Good Faith in International Law* (1991)

OECD, *National Treatment for Foreign-Controlled Enterprises* (1991)

Peter Oliver, *Free Movement of Goods in the European Community* (1996)

David Palmeter and Petros Mavroidis, *Dispute Settlement in the World Trade Organisation* (1999)

Joost Pauwelyn, "Evidence, Proof and Persuasion in WTO Dispute Settlement: Who Bears the Burden?", 1 *Journal of International Economic Law* (1998) 227

Joost Pauwelyn, "The WTO Agreement on SPS Measures as Applied in the First Three SPS Disputes", 2 *Journal of International Economic Law* (1999) 641

Ernst-Ulrich Petersmann, "Violation Complaints and Non-Violation Complaints in Public International Trade Law", 34 *German Yearbook of International Law* (1991) 175

Don Regan, "The Dormant Commerce Clause and 'Dumb Duck Disease' ", paper presented at the World Trade Forum 2000 conference "The Role of the Judge: Lessons for the WTO"

Peter Robson, *The Economics of International Integration* (4th edn., 1998)

Frieder Roessler, "Diverging Domestic Policies and Multilateral Trade Integration", in Jagdish Bhagwati and Robert Hudec (eds.) *Fair Trade and Harmonisation 1, Vol. 2* (1996)

Frieder Roessler, "Increasing Market Access under Regulatory Heterogeneity: The Strategies of the World Trade Organisation", in OECD (ed.) *Regulatory Reform and International Market Openness* (1996) 117

—— "The Concept of Nullification and Impairment in the Legal System of the World Trade Organisation", in Ernst-Ulrich Petersmann (ed.) *International Trade Law and the GATT/WTO Dispute Settlement System* (1997)

Jim Rollo and Alan Winters, "Domestic Regulation and Trade: Subsidiarity and Governance Challenges for the WTO", paper presented at the WTO/World Bank Conference on Developing Countries and the Millenium Round, Geneva, 20–21 September 1999, 1

Malcolm Ross, "Article 59 and the Marketing of Financial Services", *European Law Review* (1995) 507

Pierre Schlag, "Rules and Standards", 33 *UCLA Law Review* (1985) 379

Steven Shavell, "Strict Liability versus Negligence", 9 *Journal of Legal Studies* (1980) 1

Richard Snape, "Principles in Trade in Services", in Patrick Messerlin and Karl Sauvant (eds.) *The Uruguay Round. Services in the World Economy* (1990) 5

James Snelson, "Can Article III recover from its Head-On Collision with United States—Taxes on Automobiles?", 5 *Minnesota Journal of Global Trade* (1996) 467

Tycho H.E. Stahl, "Liberalizing International Trade in Services: The Case for Sidestepping the GATT", 19 *Yale Journal of International Law* (1994) 405

Terence Stewart, *The Uruguay Round: A Negotiating History* (1993)

Geert Straetmans, "Case Note: Alpine Investments", 2 *Columbia Journal of European Law* (1996) 154

Alan Sykes, *Product Standards for Internationally Integrated Goods Markets* (1995) 78

—— "The (Limited) Role of Regulatory Harmonisation in International Goods and Services Markets", 2 *Journal of International Economic Law* (1999) 49

Giuseppe Tesauro, "The Community's Internal Market in the Light of the recent Case Law of the Court of Justice", *Yearbook of European Law* (1995) 1

Joel Trachtman, "Trade in Financial Services under GATS, NAFTA and the EC: A Regulatory Jurisdiction Analysis", 34 *Columbia Journal of Transnational Law* (1995) 37

—— "Trade and . . . Problems, Cost-Benefit Analysis and Subsidiarity", 9 *European Journal of International Law* (1998) 32

—— "The Domain of WTO Dispute Resolution", 40 *Harvard International Law Journal* (1999) 333

Michael Trebilcock and Robert Howse, "Trade Liberalisation and Regulatory Diversity: Reconciling Competitive Markets with Competitive Politics", 6 *European Journal of Law and Economics* (1998) 5

United Nations Centre on Transnational Corporations, *Key Concepts in International Investment Arrangements and their Relevance to Negotiations on International Transactions in Services* (1990)

Gaetan Verhoosel, "Foreign Direct Investment and Legal Constraints on Domestic Environmental Policies: Striking a 'Reasonable' Balance Between Stability and Change", 29 *Georgetown Journal of Law and Policy in International Business* (1998) 451

—— and Todd Friedbacher, "Private Party Access to the WTO Dispute Settlement System: A Few Pragmatic Thoughts", paper presented at the "Regulatory Framework of Globalisation" Conference, Barcelona, October 2001.

Edwin Vermulst, Petros Mavroidis, Paul Waer, "The Functioning of the Appellate Body after Four Years: Towards Rule Integrity", 33 *Journal of World Trade* (1999) 1

David Vogel, *Trading Up: Consumer and Environmental Regulation in a Global Economy* (1993) 14

Walter van Gerven, "Articles 30, 48, 52 and 59 after *Keck and Mithouard*, and Protection of Rights arising from Directives after *Faccini Dori*", 2 *Columbia Journal of European Law* (1996) 217

Armin von Bogdandy, "The Non-Violation Procedure of Article XXIII:2(b): Its Operational Rationale", 26 *Journal of World Trade* (1992) 95

Jeffrey Waincymer, "Reformulated Gasoline under Reformulated WTO Dispute Settlement Procedures: Pulling Pandora out of a Chapeau?", 18 *Michigan Journal of International Law* (1996) 141

Stephen Weatherill, "Recent Case Law concerning the Free Movement of Goods: Mapping the Frontiers of Market Deregulation", 36 *Common Market Law Review* (1999) 51

Joseph Weiler, "The Transformation of Europe", 100 *Yale Law Journal* (1991) 2403

Friedl Weiss, "The General Agreement on Trade in Services 1994", 32 *Common Market Law Review* (1995) 1177

Serena Wille, "Recapturing a Lost Opportunity: Article III:2 GATT 1994. Japan—Taxes on Alcoholic Beverages 1996", retrievable at the *European Journal of International Law* Website, www.ejil.org

Wouter Wils, "The Search for the Rule in Article 30 EEC: Much Ado About Nothing?", *European Law Review* (1993) 475

David Wirth, "The Role of Science in the Uruguay Round and NAFTA Trade Disciplines", 27 *Cornell International Law Journal* (1994) 817

World Trade Organization, *The Results of the Uruguay Round of Multilateral Trade Negotiations* (1994)

—— *Non-Violation Complaints under Article XXIII:2, MTN.GNG/NG13/W/31*

—— *Non-Violation Complaints and the TRIPS Agreement, IP/C/W/124* (1999)

X, "The International Regulation of Foreign Direct Investment: Obstacles and Evolution", 31 *Cornell International Law Journal* (1998) 455

Americo B. Zampetti and Pierre Sauve, "New Dimensions of Market Access: An Overview", in Pierre Sauve and Americo B. Zampetti (eds.) *New Dimensions of Market Access in a Globalising World Economy* (1995) 13

Werner Zdouc, "WTO Dispute Settlement Practice Relating to the GATS", 4 *Journal of International Economic Law* (1999) 295

Rex Zedalis, "A Theory of the GATT 'Like' Product Common Language Cases", 27 *Vanderbilt Journal of Transnational Law* (1994) 33

Elisabeth Zoller, *La Bonne Foi en Droit International Public* (1977)

Index

National Treatment (*cont.*):
  integrated necessity test (*cont.*):
    necessity, 8–9, 35–8
    predictability, 71
    transparency, 72–3
    Vienna Convention, 75–101
  interpretation of provisions, 3
  legitimate policy exceptions, 64–71, 92–5
  "less favourable treatment", 21–3
  licensing and qualification require-
    ments, 95–8
  likeness:
    aims and effects test, 53
    case law, 52–64
    generally, 23
    like products, 24–33
    like service and service suppliers, 33–4
    so as to afford protection, 24–33
  non-violation complaint, 40–4, 95–101
  ordinary meaning of provisions, 74–101
  performance of obligations, 3
  standards disciplines, 95–101
  systemic arguments, 95–101
  Vienna Convention on the Law of
    Treaties, 3, 74–101
  causation theory, 74–90
  interpretation conforming with,
    74–101
Non-discrimination:
  equating with necessity, 51–112
Non-violation complaint:
  division of labour, 100–101

function, 13
GATT provisions, 13
National Treatment, 40–4, 95–101
reason for filing, 13

Protective application:
  Appellate Body, 27

Regulatory autonomy, 51
  safeguarding, 51–2
Regulatory efficiency, 51–2

Sanitary and Phytosanitary Standards
  (SPS), Agreement on, 13–14, 98–100

Technical Barriers to Trade (TBT),
  Agreement on, 13–14, 98–100
Trade liberalisation:
  deep market integration and, 2

Vienna Convention on the Law of
  Treaties:
  National Treatment, 3, 74–101
  causation theory, 74–90

WTO:
  autonomy of members, 1, 51
  constitutional function, 2
  constitutionalisation, 1
  domestic legal orders:
    interface between, 1–10
  membership, 8